THE MINISTERING CONGREGATION

THE MINISTERING CONGREGATION

by
Browne Barr and Mary Eakin

For Beth
"justified by faith"
and a friend besides!

November 1972

A PILGRIM PRESS BOOK

FROM UNITED CHURCH PRESS   PHILADELPHIA

Library of Congress Cataloging in Publication Data

Barr, Browne.
    The ministering congregation.

    Bibliography: p.
    1. Pastoral theology.   2. Church work.
I. Eakin Mary (Mulford) 1914–   joint author.
II. Title.
BV4011.B367   261   72–5587
ISBN 0–8298–0243–6

CONTENTS

FOREWORD

During the deeply disturbed decade of the sixties, it was often fashionable to proclaim the total irrelevancy, meaninglessness, and impending death of the churches and their ministry in local congregations. In the midst of that cacophony, Browne Barr spoke out with forthrightness and conviction about the positive place and necessities of the local church's ministry in an often confused and confusing world. His "Bury the Parish?" question raised in *The Christian Century* elicited a degree and extent of response that should have told us something about what was "out there." Clergy and lay persons alike found in this statement a sympathetic and supportive voice for their convictions and beliefs. Moreover, it was a position that bespoke strength and assurance rather than defensive posturing.

In a new decade, it is becoming clear just how significant that statement was for the future. Now Browne Barr and his co-minister, Mary Eakin, have brought together at the publisher's invitation the larger story of the ministering church in our time. It is a story that is both reflective and active, one that moves back and forth between biblical and theological convictions and specific events in the life of a local church. To them this story is their congregation's story. Characteristic

9

of their abiding belief and practice in such a community, at the time of contracting for this book they signed over all its royalties to the Berkeley church they serve because "it is really their book."

The Ministering Congregation is a positive statement about the role and future of the local church and it shows some of the ways in which local clergy and lay people can strengthen and vitalize a church's life. The authors are convinced that the pressing need of American Christianity is for a strengthening and renewal of the ministry of all believers. Excessive concern with activism, specialized ministries, and criticism from above or from the sidelines has seriously impaired and confused the issues. At the same time, the authors are wisely and prudently concerned that the call for primary attention to the local church not become an excuse behind which to hide. The local church "must stand up and be heard and share its experience and make its claim and bear its responsibility."

These chapters depict a variety of elements of the ministering congregation and speak about its responsibilities. As such they are intimately related to one another and have developed from a common set of convictions. The common threads that consistently appear and tie the parts together include a clear statement of the standard of the gospel of Jesus Christ for all that is undertaken as ministry, the tremendous significance of finding an openness to receive the Holy Spirit in our time, a conviction that the church is fundamentally an institution of Tradition, Book, and Gospel, that activism apart from religious experience is an empty and hollow thing for the church, and that the Christian ministry is preeminently a ministry of all believers.

The authors make clear the vital difference between the *substance* and the *consequences* of ministry. Here is a source of confusion that became preeminent in the sixties and threatens to continue its troublesome disruption in the seventies.

Browne Barr and Mary Eakin find that the important work of the church, indeed its raison d'être, is not found in its location or its constituency but in its *character*, which is determined by its gospel. And so, what should ministers be doing in these "revolutionary times" or any times? First and foremost, "preach the gospel, administer the sacraments, and bear rule in the church." The essentials are determined by "Christ's coming, as he has promised, where two or three are gathered together in his name." And thus "if the church does not show forth the dimensions of the eternal in its common life, how will it—let alone the world—know its Lord or feel the demands and comfort of perfect love?"

The Ministering Congregation speaks of those demands and the assurance of that comfort both in terms of a broad framework for understanding and in terms of the specific consequences thereof. To keep the two together is essential and thus the book moves back and forth between them. The thoughtful and useful measurement of Ephesians 4:11–12 is broken open and consistently applied throughout these pages. Ultimately it binds them together just as it is perceived as binding together the community of believers. Finally, here is an exciting story of the pilgrimage of a people. It is a pilgrimage of struggle and temptation, but it is also a pilgrimage of discovery and hope and joy. And thus the reader is left with the authors' clear conviction that it will all be worthwhile if only the effort is made.

The Publisher

THE MINISTERING CONGREGATION

INTRODUCTION

The sanitation department in an Arizona city was stymied recently. In an economy move it sought to reduce the number of stops each collection truck would have to make by providing larger barrels to be shared by two families. At once they were confronted with great resistance by the householders. Some wise person solved the problem by arranging for three or more families to share each barrel. The resistance had arisen, so it appears, because if only two households used each barrel, one would know that anything he saw in the trash collection which he had not contributed had come from the other. With three or more contributing, that certainty was removed and you could not be sure who was responsible.

If the same psychology prevails, it would seem unwise to offer a book which brings together separate offerings of only two authors. Each one could always assign credit or blame where it suited his own dark purposes. However, we have not risked such an enterprise. This volume reflects the wisdom of that unknown sage of the sanitation department. Into its barrel many persons have made contributions. (We have probably reached the safe edge of the trash collection metaphor!) We wish to make clear that this volume is a book originating in a Christian congregation. Its life together has produced certain important, inescapable themes which recur with consistency throughout the chapters which follow. Whether we are telling the story of how this congregation determined a "life style for the 70's" (chapter 4) or pressing for change in theological education (chapter 8), the congregation's wisdom is there.

Certain threads will be found weaving in and out through the entire fabric: themes such as the insistence that the church must at all times be aware of its centering in Christ and of its charge to remain open, obedient, and faithful to his living spirit, and the recognition that true religion is a lively excitation, e-motive, that is, moving men and women into action as an inevitable moral response to hearing and receiving the gospel. The chapters will readily be found to rest on the understanding that Christianity is based on knowledge derived from experience (history) more than on knowledge drawn from reason (philosophy); and that it is, therefore, inescapably social, carried through persons *in community* and ministering to persons *in community* and never wholly individual though indeed profoundly personal. If the writers report extensively on the experience of one congregation, this of itself supports the contention that the church is always a particular community gathered for worship and witness in a particular place, and that this community of faith is called into being in order to be the redemptive agency of Christ. Therefore, the primary function of professional theological schools is taken to be the preparation of men and women for ministry with local congregations; and the function of the minister is presented as that of enabler of the congregation for *its* work, namely, to be Christ's presence in the world.

We offer this book not as some final wisdom but with the hope of encouraging other local congregations to engage in conversation about specific, practical ways to refresh the church in its "local aspect" while keeping it faithful to its centering in Christ. The local church is the particular concern and bias of this book not because it is the *only* aspect of the church, but because it is the one on which a congregation is most competent to report. We also press such a concern and bias in this year of our Lord because there is evidence that it has been seriously neglected of late.

Of course the day is long past when any congregation can preserve the illusion of absolute autonomy, as though it did not need other churches and could deny its national and international manifestations. A local church in Southern California has a big, bold sign under its name reading: "This Is a Free and Independent Church." Nonsense! There is no such thing in Christendom. Yet, there is a local *aspect* to the church much in need of nurturing because it is fundamental to all the rest: councils, theological schools, conferences, mission boards, ad infinitum. But it is not enough for local churches to scold that they have been overlooked by councils and schools and then behave like forgotten and rejected parents pouting in their old age. The local congregation must stand up and be heard and share its experience and make its claim and bear its responsibility.

Years ago that eminent British Congregationalist theologian, P. T. Forsyth, wrote: "Episcopacy stands for the Church's welfare and freedom as secured by *authority*. Presbyterianism stands for it as secured by *order*. And Congregationalism stands for it as secured by local *autonomy and initiative*."[1] It may, therefore, be fitting for a congregation whose heritage in the United Church of Christ and in the larger ecumenical scene is linked with Forsyth and New England Congregationalism to make the effort to restate the importance of the local aspect of the church before the whole church. But this can become a narrow and provincial concern if it proposes the local church as an end in itself. This peril may be avoided by bearing in heart and mind further words of Dr. Forsyth in the same connection:

This last (the local aspect) is committed to our charge—a warm, lay and ethical localism. To make a thing living make it local. To develop local initiative give local responsibility under a large and free control. Think of local responsibility instead of local privilege, excellence or preeminence. But realize that these three polities are members one of another. They are good for each other. They are all contributory to the fulness of the body of Christ, and complementary to its glory.[2]

We do not know whether the Episcopalians and the Presbyterians would agree with Dr. Forsyth's analysis of their particular excellences. But our congregation knows that in wrestling with the problems of the local aspect of the church we have been mightily assisted by our neighboring churches of those and other denominations. With them we have participated in a "warm, lay and ethical localism" in an ecumenical cluster of churches. We have been led to see the opportunities for the different congregations to expand not only by joint enterprises but also as each has helped the other to examine, develop, and show forth its distinctive and complementary style of parish life. This subject would require another book or two. But two things are clear from that growing experience in local ecumenicity: (1) weakened local churches do not enhance the ecumenical movement; (2) local churches are not necessarily strengthened by coming together out of practical necessity rather than by religious necessity.

So this book has many contributors. They are mostly unnamed. We hope that the volume will provoke fruitful and creative conversation in many congregations and that out of it may come other more complete and useful work for the renewal of the church.

It is important to make clear that the present writers have

presumed on their own to speak for the congregation, to reflect what they think the congregation is saying and would say if it could to fellow Christians. But we are also speaking for other professional colleagues in the church, especially for the Rev. Fred Strasburg who has been engaged with us for over ten years in the ministry of this particular congregation, for the Rev. Albert Kissling who in three years time has done much to prod our thinking and to expand our experience, and for all the members of the ministering team, lay and ordained alike, who have been busy on other parts of our shared ministry while we have pulled these chapters together.

The division of writing is reflected in our somewhat different styles of writing. Chapters 1, 2, 3, 5, 7, and 8 were originally written by Browne Barr and chapters 4, 6, and 9 by Mary Eakin. Although we have jointly revised them, we have thought it better to let these chapters bear their unique marks whereas the whole book is the result of our common endeavors and ministry in Berkeley, California.

These chapters would never have made it into this binding without the help of our gentle office disciplinarian, Mary E. Campbell, who sat at her desk, typewriter unsheathed, dictionary open, tapping her fingers impatiently when we dawdled. She kept us moving and in line as she has our whole parish for almost thirty years.

Browne Barr

Mary Eakin

CHAPTER 1

RETOOLING FOR
A NEW STYLE

A family in our church now spanning several generations and several continents is well known for its unusual zest for life and its creative spirit. Recently one of the oldest members died, and as we left the cemetery his sister said she had something to show me. She had come upon a journal started over sixty years ago, just before their father and mother were married. It is in their father's handwriting and sets forth the style of life which he hoped would characterize the home and family soon to be established.

It shall be a home of the old school rich in tradition, custom and blessed days. . . . There shall be grace before meals, thanking devoutly Him from whom we receive daily our lives and all the happiness thereof. Every week shall bring some glad trip to a beautiful place in our Father's estate where we refresh our souls. . . . Daily we shall read from some great book expanding our lives and filling our lungs with the pure air of stories rich in truth and goodness.

So the style of a family was established and the grown children, now parents and grandparents themselves, discovering this journal after the death of both parents, are amazed to note how persistent the style thus determined was in their parents' home and how much of it remains in their own.

If you examine this declaration carefully, you discover two elements interwoven in it which together make up that family's style. First, the *intention*, the goal; and second, some *ritual* by which it may be achieved. For example, "God shall be devoutly thanked"; that is the intention. Therefore, there shall be grace before meals. That is the ritual ordered: intention—ritual. Or again, "We shall refresh our souls from nature"; that is the intention. Therefore, "each week shall bring some glad trip to a beautiful place"; that is the ritual. Intention—ritual. These two fused together created a style of life.

The letter to the Colossians is also a journal of sorts in which some early father of the church set forth a style of life which he hoped would characterize the congregation he addressed. In the third chapter he proposed the same combination of intention and ritual for building that style of life. The intention was put forth: "Let Christ's teaching live in your hearts, making you rich in the true wisdom." That is central, abiding, unchanging yet. But to be incorporated into a life style it needs a ritual. So the text continues, "Teach and help one another along the right road with your psalms and hymns and Christian songs." So Christian meeting, study, celebration, worship. Christian ritual is suggested and the two together, intention and ritual, create a style of life which the writer devoutly trusted would make the Christian community adequate for the day in which it lived.

So styles of life are created by and for families and congregations. *But new days call for new styles.* The family of the man who wrote the journal is now grown and spread to the four corners of the world. It can no longer get together for the ritual of a weekly trip to a beautiful place. It has had to give that up under the pressure of other circumstances and inevitable changes. But woe to that family if it also surrenders the intention—the refreshment of soul. A new ritual to implement that intention must be found or all that will be left is a style of

life in which a diminishing number can participate creatively.

In many places Christian congregations are burdened with a style of corporate life—Sunday school and eleven o'clock worship service and afternoon teas, Christian Endeavor and foreign missionary societies—a style which is no longer vital. There is nothing wrong with the intention they hold. It is as unchanging as God's love, but the form of their life together, their ritual, is dated, and the resulting style of life is a period piece—of interest to antiquarians but of no present vitality.

Now that ritual to which we are sometimes tempted to cling as though *it were the intention* was functional when it was designed. It filled the need and suited the times. But it was a time before television and professional football and an express highway to ski slopes. It was a time when the moral assumptions of the church were widely shared in society, and no one thought anything about it if a teacher prayed in a public school in the name of Christ. It was a time when the editor of a newspaper in every city of size was acquainted with the pastor, and public officials participated in the value structure of the church. From such times we have retained rituals and forms in which a declining number of people continue doggedly to participate out of a sense of duty but which are not styled to contemporary life. The church wants to believe that modern man is out of step with the church; that may be quite true as far as *intention* is concerned. But as far as form and ritual are concerned it may be better to investigate the possibility that the church is out of step with modern man. Many young people leave the church not because Christianity seems to them untrue, not because its intention is not valid, but because its forms are inadequate and its ritual a bore. So Ignazio Silone writes: "One fine Sunday some of us stopped going to Mass, not because Catholic dogma seemed to us, all of a sudden, false, but because the people who went began to bore us and we were drawn to the company of those who stayed away." [1]

The time is long since upon us for retooling to create a new and vital life style for Christian congregations. It is a difficult task because institutions which help provide stability to life as the church must are notably and necessarily resistant to change.

Consider now how crucial is our philosophy and method of restyling. Some seek restyling like the 1957 Chevrolet. The 1955 model was innovative and had integrity; the 1956 offered a few minor changes; but in 1957, in an effort to create new interest and new sales with little expense, the designers simply tampered here and there with the basic 1955 model, adding more chrome, an extra hood ornament, and silly fins. It was a monstrous creation. We Protestants have been approaching our sagging life style in pretty much the same fashion. We have added a few frills to meet some odd demand or tried the sensational or the spectacular or added something for *aesthetic* reasons, and the result has been atrocious.

Others in the church, rightly impatient with tampering, have tried fundamental restyling like the 1935 Airflow Chrysler and DeSoto. These models, you may recall, were radically redesigned, following the practical implications of aerodynamics. The theory was correct and the models were technical marvels years ahead of their time, but that retooling proved almost disastrous to the Chrysler Corporation. The break with traditional style was too abrupt. They didn't consult the market. The technicians overlooked the human limitations which are part of the equation. So also in our time many who would bring a ritual of the church up-to-date are quite right historically and theoretically in their proposals, but somehow people who have attended church at 11:00 A.M. for years in their Sunday best and have sung "Holy, Holy, Holy" and have entertained visiting missionaries are resistant to a jazz mass at midnight with a barefoot minister playing a guitar.

What happened in 1933 or 1934 to the restyling of Fisher Bodies by General Motors may be a better guide. There was introduced a radical change in the windows of sedan models. They were literally cut in two vertically and at first glance appeared unseemly and difficult to operate. But this change came about in response to the demand for better ventilation, so you could have a window open and not be blown in the face. This was the first so-called no-draft ventilation and has long since been standard on almost all automobiles until recently when air conditioning altered the situation. This styling change came as the designers saw ordinary people holding cardboard up to the open window to deflect the wind. The people knew what they needed and had the right approach. The designers were wise enough to follow the lead thus provided. They did not violate the theoretical principles of their training or abandon their professional expertise by listening to the consumer. Rather, they listened to the expressed need and sought to meet it with something far more sound and lasting and effective than the untrained cardboard-holder alone could have provided.

In subsequent chapters we shall seek to set forth some theological principles particularly pertinent in restyling congregational life and to suggest some methods for implementing them especially appropriate for twentieth-century American Protestantism and its leadership. Consider first, in broad strokes, the possible creative and professional response of church leadership to one need expressed in numerous ways in a variety of congregations today. Ecclesiastical cardboard-holders in the modern pew (and all too often recently out of it) are expressing a genuine need of sorts when they deplore controversy and seek to avoid conflict in the church, because they want a place of shelter from life's storms and the solace of a religious community marked by care for one another rather than by bitterness, jealousy, and divisiveness. At once we sense the dangers and the legitimacies of that request. Restyling the church cannot ignore the real human hunger thus expressed.

Responsible professional leadership will build on that expression and not simply be threatened by it.

Whenever I hear this need expressed I am reminded of the suggestion made by Richard E. Wentz that the church as an institution must develop the umbrella principle. Our first response may be: Well, that is about all we need—the image of an umbrella—to suggest that the church is a shelter from the storms of life, a place where people can hide from the realities of the pelting rain and skin-lashing winds and bruising hail. "Come on in under my umbrella! We will pretend that the whole world is like it is here—dry and safe!"

Such a response hardly does justice to umbrellas, for when you stop to think of it an umbrella is what makes it possible for you to forsake the security of four walls and venture out *into* the storm; an umbrella provides you with mobility despite the storms, it is in league with you against them, it helps you to go on even when the skies are dark and the sun is hiding and the rain is coming down.

It is often self-defeating to push any figure of speech too far, as many a preacher has learned to his sorrow and his congregation's amusement. Already I can imagine someone starting down his own imaginary path with visions of useless, decorative parasols or umbrellas blown inside out by a single, strong gust. Nonetheless, this figure of speech has been very helpful to us in our Berkeley congregation in holding together in an increasingly flexible way a diverse congregation. It has given us a simple figure of speech to make clear a mutually agreed upon style for our parish life. It has helped mightily in the bridging of many gaps—town-gown, generation-generation, black-white. It has been useful even to the point of an appropriate rebuke when a layman pointed out the peril of hanging the umbrella up as the church's ultimate symbol replacing the cross.

The figure can be employed only as we note some unchang-

26

ing characteristics of the umbrella we call the church. First, it will help to think of the church in this way only if we understand that it is a *very, very, large umbrella.* Paul was not speaking of any parasol just large enough for me and mine and a couple of other people I find especially congenial (such is the peril of the "neighborhood" church as well as the "issue-oriented" church) when he wrote, "For as in one body we have many members, and all the members do not have the same function, so we, though many, are one body in Christ (Rom. 12:4–5)."

But we Protestants are caught up in a cultural identity situation where through historical necessity and human sin the church has appeared as an umbrella only large enough for people who share a common style of life or racial background or political persuasion. This is understandable because our faith has rested as much in the church supper as in the Lord's Supper, and it is easier to have that sort of fellowship with people you like. But that is a very narrow experience. It makes a mockery of the grand dimension of humanity revealed in Jesus Christ and seriously handicaps his work of reconciliation and peace.

Last summer a minister friend of mine appeared one day wearing a clerical collar, psychedelic beads, a peace symbol, and a Rotary lapel button. There is nothing *ultimate* about any of the values expressed by those symbols. In the church they must be brought together by a faith which transcends them all. To be so inclusive is not to be spineless but magnificently strong and open. It was no little man eager to please everybody who wrote, "I have become all things to all men, that I might by all means save some."

The new form and shape of the church for an increasingly pluralistic society must be a form and shape which provides for people to come to Christ in diverse ways in worship and fellowship and involvement in the world. It must also be a place where the common faith of separated generations and different personalities can be expressed and understanding increased. So then we must note that if it helps to think of the church as an umbrella, we must remember that it is a very, very, large umbrella.

Come then, and note in the second place that it is only helpful to think of the church as an umbrella if we remember that it is *one we have borrowed*. It is not ours. We did not dream it up or create it or design it or purchase it. It is not *ours* at all and therefore we are not free to do with it as we please.

If we had designed it we might have made it smaller. That would be easier. It would remove a lot of the headaches and we could snuggle under it as though it were a private club; we could judge it by our standards of congeniality or comfort. But there is a tremendous givenness to the church. Its boundaries are set by the gospel; its goals were projected on a mountain in Galilee; its tradition is established and its heroes are defined by the prophets, apostles, and martyrs. The tempo to which it marches when it really moves is sounded by some drummer other than the one the world hears.

It is a great temptation when the going is rough and congregations are restless and youth are alienated for Christians, in their effort to make the church relevant and help it to be "with it," to try to reshape it according to their own wisdom, to return the borrowed umbrella and fashion one with more flair, reflecting some norm other than the one given in its own history and its own inheritance. As the traditionalists may tend to make the umbrella too small and mistake the church for a private club, so the innovators, now in the ascendancy in liberal Protestant circles, may tend to persuade us to forget that the umbrella is borrowed—it is not our own.

Theological education, once centered in theology and Bible, was pressed for relevancy and so developed essential derivative studies in education, sociology, psychology. But now it is confronted by students, rightly determined to participate in their own education, who have been unwisely persuaded that what is derivative is primary and what is primary is "old hat," and the church is left with an increasing number of ministers equipped with little to help the church's dialogue with the world save the world's own wisdom. The same has been true in the preparation of children and adults for church membership: they possess no grounding in the historical and intellectual substance of the faith and are inarticulate about the tradition they are charged to pass on to the next generation. As that umbrella is borrowed so must it be handed on, and the true apostolic succession may be that suggested by J. S. Whale, the British Congregationalist: "Jesus loves me, this I know, for my mother told me so." [2]

If the church be our own construction, it will be of small help in getting us through the storm of these years. But even that most severe critic of the local church, sociologist Peter Berger, who scored it hard a few years ago in his book *The Noise of Solemn Assemblies,* now sees the churches as conservators "of what has been most precious and most humane in American civilization." Under this umbrella we may be able to move against the storm for as Berger also reminds us "the principal moral benefit of religion is that it permits a confrontation with the age in which one lives in a perspective that transcends that age and thus puts it in proportion." [3] Such perspective, a place out of the storm while in the midst of it, is the admirable service of an umbrella—especially this large, borrowed one.

Finally, if it is helpful to think of the church as an umbrella, not only must we remember that it is a very, very large one and that it is borrowed—no matter how much we covet its paraphernalia in buildings and bylaws—but also that *those who share its liberating shelter must help hold it up and keep it open.*

We are immediately confronted with the danger of suggesting that the church really is man's and not God's, and that if we don't help hold it up it will collapse. That's not what this borrowed umbrella looks like that has come down through the centuries. It has suffered incredible neglect and abuse at the hands of men and it has survived. Yet, it must be admitted also that there have been dark, dim days in its history, days of opulence and wealth and perversion and corruption when it has all but folded up. We know it is God's or it would have collapsed under the pressure of human sin centuries ago, blown inside out by the fury of human folly. But it is also clear that its renewal has come as men have been open to God's power and have stretched her limp canvas tight once more and straightened out her stays and broadened her protecting, guiding reach. But for neither layman nor minister is it held up just by brute force, by resolve or exhortation but by reality of religious experience.

So the question Paul Tillich set forth before his death is the primary one for us to face as we consider any restyling of the church for the 70's. He said the question "What shall we do?" should be answered with another question: "Whence can we receive?" He then suggested the need for people to learn they must receive before they will be able to act. Finally, he proposed that religion ought to be thought of as receiving a gift (from God) and then giving gifts (to others).

Well, we have done pretty well in distributing such as we have received, but we are no longer receiving much. Has the source of supply been cut off? Is God withholding his Spirit and the gifts he brings? Our young people are going elsewhere in a desperate, disguised search for these gifts—meaning, harmony, peace, spiritual experience, beauty, love, direction. College graduates flood into the mystic cults—yoga, drugs, communes. And our older people have already settled down in other pastures for less: in clubs and commercial absorption and in the meaning that money provides, in style, in propriety, and in the comforts of conformity. But what of the gifts of the Spirit, the promises of Christ? "I will not leave you desolate; I will come to you. Yet a little while, and the world will see me no more, but you will see me; because I live, you will live also (John 14:18-19)." So it was when the first believers, the first people touched by his life, came together to talk about him and reason together over these events. "They were all filled with the Holy Spirit." They knew its liberating power. So religion is being open to receive a gift.

> Ransomed, healed, restored, forgiven,
> Who, like me, his praise should sing? [4]

Why do we so seldom receive such glorious gifts? Has God really died? Has his Holy Spirit deserted us? Or is there some inadequacy, some inability in *us?* It seems more modest and appropriate and faithful to suspect that the problem is in us, in modern man, children of the enlightenment. This problem will not be resolved by oratory from the pulpit, or by Bible reading, or small-group discussion, or contemporized liturgies until all these activities are transformed for us by discovering that we have been using only half our capacity to receive the Spirit. We are wonderfully equipped to receive what God presents, but we are children of an age of rationalism and skepticism which has proudly and vainly trusted only one part of the God-given equipment. It is as though we possessed perfectly good television sets but stubbornly held to the belief that only the picture was to be trusted—seeing is believing— and turned off the sound altogether, announcing to the world "you can't believe what you hear," pressing the assumption that it was unreal, phony, an illusion, not to be trusted.

In an exciting and extremely important paper on Christianity and symbolic realism, Prof. Robert Bellah, of the Uni-

31

versity of California, reminds us that this view assumes that the reality we are dealing with resides in the object, out there (objective reality), a view which also suggests, on the other hand, that the word subjective is considered synonymous with "unreal, untrue, fallacious." [5] This so-called objectiveness, the curse of our time, the mind-set of an age of science, has closed down at least half our receiving apparatus to the gift of the Spirit. Michael Polanyi, a philosopher of science, writes earnestly that such "objectivism has totally falsified our conception of truth, by exalting what we can know and *prove*, while covering up with ambiguous utterances all that we know and *cannot* prove" [6]—like the triumphant power of beauty and loyalty and prayer.

Down where we come face to face with our infinite weakness and the knowledge of our inevitable death, there at the edge of all being, the Eternal is met. If there, in that universal human storm, we find shelter in his church and encouragement from Christ, assurance of eternal love and knowledge of our forgiveness, then we are possessed by such joy that we cannot help jumping to our feet and holding up the umbrella, making it large and loving, and moving it out to receive everyone who will come.

One summer, driving through a rural area, we heard a gospel singer call out a song, "I've just got religion and I can't sit down." Well, I should say so! The ritual was different from the ritual styled for most of us. It wasn't very much like a Bach chorale and its stanzas didn't match Luther's verse, but it spoke a plain Christian truth of the excitement which comes as soul supports soul in the fulfilling of God's intention for his church. Its intention was clear: share the gospel. No style could match it unless it was marked by joy.

So—"Let Christ's teaching live in your hearts, making you rich in true wisdom. Teach and help one another along the right road with your psalms and hymns and Christian songs (Col. 3:16, PHILLIPS [7])."

CHAPTER 2

BURY THE PARISH?

All across Western Christendom there are little community centers. They possess buildings and people and money. There is scarcely a neighborhood in slum or suburb or rural area that is without such a center, small or large, creative or corrupt. These centers are often weak, depleted, wicked, irrelevant, impoverished in spirit, and rich in things. But their potential is tremendous for, however deep their corruption, not one of them is without a tradition and a book and a gospel, hidden or exposed. These little communities await leadership, revival, direction to release the gospel they hold for the world's redemption. They are parish churches.

There are two schools of thought in regard to the proper way of dealing with them. One is the conservative approach; it says, "Let well enough alone." The church reminds us of much that is good. Keep the hymns singing and the meetings meeting and let those come who will, but don't try to change it, don't touch it. The other is the radical approach; it insists that it is high time the last labored breath were stifled and the funeral service held so that we can get on with more important matters. Let us develop relevant ministries and stop waving the hand of a corpse at the passersby to assure them that all is well. That body was suited only to the rural culture of an age long since dead. Bury it.

It is my conviction that the traditional churchman—especially if he is a layman over fifty years old—tends to the conservative approach, and the professional leadership of mainline Protestantism, apart from the parish clergy, tends to the radical approach. Neither approach is viable; one rests in the past, the other lives in the future, and both try to avoid the present. There is, however, a middle ground.

During his 1932 campaign for the Presidency, Franklin Roosevelt declared that "civilization is a tree which, as it grows, continually produces rot and dead wood." "The radical," he went on, "says, 'Cut it down.' The conservative says, 'Don't touch it.' The liberal compromises, 'Let's prune it, so that we lose neither the old trunk nor the new branches.' " This third position is congenial to the temper of the parish minister who, despite the disappointments and the resistance of the American parish, does not lose his conviction that the church is an agent for social betterment. Such a minister recognizes further that betterment is served not only by dramatic action, but also by bringing into focus that purposeful stability which gives impetus to constructive change but challenges that which is demonic and destructive.

How to find that middle ground? George Macleod has a pointer for us. As a scout officer in open warfare during World War I, he tells us he hourly received from the scouts and from the main body to the rear what he terms "messages of contradictory indignation." "The scouts asserted we moved too slow; the Colonel that we moved too fast. If, by evening, these remonstrances were equal I assumed we were in the right place." The parish minister will recognize those messages and understand Macleod's operating theory. It is a theory that should be congenial also to dialecticians, theological or materialistic.

34

A MIDDLE GROUND

Of course, the men who are working out this theory in terms of parish community life in the suburbs and slums of the nation do not have all the angels standing in their middle ground. But if this middle ground be not held, what then? It is well observed that the reactionary and the radical have much in common. They are alike, for example, in their inability to live in the present. They are alike in their disdain for the great agencies of cultural stability—the Constitution, the courts, the church. The radical left once saw their dreams of reforms frustrated by the "nine old men" of the Supreme Court; more recently the radical right wanted to "impeach Earl Warren." So also in relation to the parish church. In many congregations and in many "religious" publications two identifiable dissenting groups are represented. One would like to worship before a Christ in the image of John Birch; the other would feel more comfortable worshiping in a science laboratory or in a tavern decorated with kinetic sculpture painted pink.

Can a case be made for the middle ground—for pruning the tree, for moving slowly, the while patiently holding together the hastening front and the dragging rear of the Lord's parish army? I believe there can. Timely reminders come from the fundamental thrust of the Old Testament and the New. One Old Testament truth which the reactionary wing of today's church has tended to obscure is this: the Christian faith is a social phenomenon. This fact of Christian experience is underlined by our finding no incongruity in a "sociology of religion." British Congregationalist P. T. Forsyth, ignored for two generations or more while we shifted the gospel to individual shoulders, put it nicely:

It is quite true that the Church begins empirically, practically, with the individual, but it does not end there. And ideally, spiritually, it does not even begin there, for it was a race that Christ redeemed, and not a mere bouquet of believers. It was a Church He saved, and not a certain pale of souls. Each soul is saved in a universal and corporate salvation.[1]

We are not permitted the luxury of choosing to have Christian faith in isolation, to receive it individually and alone. It is a community affair. The community precedes Christ and the birthday of the church far predates Pentecost, no matter what the prayer book or the Sunday school curriculum proposes. The church is a community of faith, showing forth in its corporate life a certain behavior through which Christ introduces himself. The community is his agency. The people Paul set out to find in Damascus and return in chains to Jerusalem were known by their behavior, not by their doctrine (although the two are inseparable twins); they were known as "followers of the Way."

GROUPS CALLED CONGREGATIONS

So across the land the community centers called churches and peopled by groups called congregations are crucial. As Paul Tillich put it:

A church is a community of those who affirm that Jesus is the Christ. The very name "Christ" implies this. For the individual, this means a decision—not as to whether he, personally, can accept the assertion that Jesus is the Christ, but the decision as to whether he wishes to belong or not to belong to a community which asserts that Jesus is the Christ.[2]

That is a helpful hint to many honorable men. We have laid upon ourselves the responsibility to make the witness and life of that community uncommonly faithful and obedient for the conversion of its own members as well as for the reconciliation of the world. Yet, although the church always confesses and affirms more than any individual—limited as he is in time and being—ever can, if the individual's belonging does not also become the occasion and circumstance of conversion, we have the spectacle of faith only in another's faith.

It is my judgment that the so-called "specialized ministries" —essential as they are and as much as they need encouragement—exist almost entirely to fill the gap created by the faithlessness of the established community of faith. These ministries, moreover, often tend to fragmentize the community and in some unfortunate instances even suggest that the community is not only unnecessary but also a hindrance to Christ. Theoretically, the only specialized ministry that cannot be gainsaid is the prison chaplaincy, for it is a ministry to the one community which, by nature, is absolutely separated from the total community. And indeed, the prison chaplaincy may well have as its chief occupation the removal of this wall and the elimination of that specialty. The other specialized ministries (often characterized, and sometimes correctly so, as the cutting edge of the church) tend to divide community: the campus ministry, ministry to night workers, to gamblers, to nightclubs, to hospital patients. To be sure, human limitations make it necessary to train persons in the skills required to show care for men and women in particular and peculiar circumstances. Every congregation should seek to train and support such persons. When any of these ministries is exercised apart from a direct, responsible, and acknowledged connection to a specific community of believers in which the word of God is preached and the sacraments are duly administered, it is in grave peril of waking up one day to find that the charismatic horse it was riding was hooked to a carousel. It went round and round stylishly to the accompaniment of pleasant sounds but finally ran out of steam and stopped where it had started.

Some years ago a specialized ministry was launched in San Francisco's North Beach, then more than now an art colony. An able, young specialized minister gathered an enthusiastic following and won much space in the daily press with his humanitarian and artistic good works and his denunciations of the parish churches that were paying his salary. The sponsoring committee agreed with the young minister that his efforts should be directed not to all of North Beach but only to its artists, for in a few years they would be molders of public opinion either as creative geniuses or as writers of television commercials. So no church was established, no community gathered, no form or structure tolerated, no parish connection acknowledged or encouraged. Presently the minister wearied of that specialty and moved away. His successor held on for a time; now he too is gone. Today in North Beach there is neither sight nor sound of Christ in any way connected with the hours and dollars spent in that specialized ministry, save as he is held in fragmented memory through his devoted servants. But he was never incarnated there because community and its essential structure were denied.

Specialized ministries are a logical counterpart to specialized congregations. Here, of course, is the valid criticism of the suburban church: it is a specialized congregation and as such is lamented and scolded. Presumably the attacks on the residential parish grow out of observation of the corruption to which the suburban parish is prone. If alienation from God is more subtle and hidden in suburbia than in Harlem, should we therefore abandon it to the Elmer Gantrys? And does the innercity parish escape residential patterns of sin? And, escape them or not, are its temptations and troubles any less severe? Certainly as far as ministers are concerned, I believe it takes as strong a prophet and patient a pastor to move into the heart of Beverly Hills or Shaker Heights as it does to move into Chicago's West Side.

Or, again, it is proposed to gather Christian community along vocational lines. What will you have: a parish made up of brokers or bakers or candlestick-makers, or of culturally deprived people, or of students? Specialized communities of faith appear not only in suburbia or in the college chapel (and both are to be regretted as probable necessities imposed by human sin) but also among people who know better. I must confess that I was shocked to learn that the World Council of Churches had built a chapel in Geneva! I suppose the chapel meets a desperate need, but what does it do to Christian community in Geneva? In Berkeley the parish church is almost the only significant and regular place of meeting for town and gown. If the university were to build a chapel, that meeting would be impoverished, as it is in many academic centers. Incidentally, I was privately amused by the report of a World Council officer stationed in Geneva who said that, once the chapel was built, he and his colleagues would no longer have to worship at their desks or pray amid paper clips and typewriters. But I thought reality in worship was part of the Secular City!

WHAT KIND OF COMMUNITY?

The parish's problems and difficulties persist, and they are intensified by residential location and vocational interest and culturally determined value structures. But none of these is the central problem. The central problem is the question of what kind of communities these parish outposts are. And the answer to that question is not primarily sociological but religious.

This brings us to the New Testament and to the truth that the authenticity and hence the authority of these communities of faith is evangelical in disposition and not theological. What is called for is not right doctrine but right faith. The evangelical authenticity and authority every congregation must possess if it is to be more than a club is elicited, secured, and cor-

39

rected by the preaching of the gospel in word and in sacrament. These marks of the church remain as indispensable agents of the Holy Spirit.

I do not mean to suggest any narrow or doctrinaire interpretation of either word or sacrament, but neither do I mean to encourage so free an interpretation that Wordsworth, or Shakespeare himself, is elevated to the status of Holy Writ. Writ is made holy not by its literary quality, nor even by its moral good sense, but by its relationship to the time and circumstance of the Divine Invasion. A historical religion is less impressed by the enduring value of great verse than by the events in personal and public history which are the source of great verse. The well trained, well educated, well disciplined parish minister is offered by the community of faith and by his own conscience as an instrument for the contemporary reenactment of that central event in history by which alone the community of faith is created and sustained. Much confusion about the role of the ordained clergy would be cleared away if the seminaries as well as the churches were not frequently so ready to forget this audacious claim and this presumptuous undertaking.

Overlooking that truth has fostered the heresy which is present wherever some consequence of the gospel, rather than the gospel itself, is put forth as the source of the church's power and vitality. In our time such heresy threatens wherever it is implied that the unity of the church is the source of its power in the world and the divisions of the church the chief evidence of its sin. Reinhold Niebuhr long since pointed out (in *Faith and History*) the absurdity of waiting for the absolute healing of the church's divisions before sharing the sacrament, but we still stubbornly try to pull the horse with the cart. Jaroslav Pelikan has reminded us of Luther's profound interpretation of church in this connection. In explaining Luther's conviction he writes:

The unity of the church is to be sought, first of all, in the gospel, and not in anything external or human. Not what a man thinks about the gospel (theology) or what he wears when he proclaims it (ritual) or how he organizes a church to proclaim it (polity), but God proclaiming the gospel through Word and sacrament brings about the unity of the church.[3]

When we make unity an absolute we ignore (as Tillich said) the spiritual necessity of the sort of criticism and reformation which often results in division. There is some genuine religious motivation for church unity in local churches, but where that unity comes about easily, it very often comes not out of obedience but out of indifference to the gospel and is prompted less by arguments theological than by arguments economical. If this be true, how urgent is the necessity for a ministry of word and sacrament, and how instant are the claims of its priority over a ministry ecumenical and specialized! For the latter can rise with authenticity only out of the former.

PARISH MINISTER

The argument I press then is this: the essential thing about the community of faith—a community which precedes the Christ and is his agent—is not its location or its constituency but its character; and that character is determined by its gospel (i.e., by Christ's coming, as he has promised, where two or three are gathered together in his name), not by the community's theology or ritual or unity or anything else. Hence the crucial role of the clergy in a church which affirms the priesthood of all believers. If the clergy abdicate this role, deny this responsibility, and neglect the community of faith and its nurture in the gospel, there will be no community left to exercise its redemptive work in and upon the alienated world. It is no little thing for a minister to decide "to take things into his own hands" and to try to be the church in the world. The specialized ministries tend to encourage him in this presumptuousness,

41

and the popular cry of dismay about the impotence of the local church affirms him in his heroism (or his martyrdom or his foolishness).

What then is the role of a parish minister in revolutionary times? My contention is that his role is "to preach the gospel, administer the sacraments, and bear rule in the church." If these are times of great social change, this role is all the more crucial. If the parish minister must neglect the flock committed to his care in order to exercise his own Christian citizenship, then one may wonder about his understanding of Christian citizenship. The failure of the parish church to attract bold and bright young men to labor in it as pastors and teachers arises largely from the urgent desire of youth to be instruments of the revolution and from their doubt about the parish church as an agent of social healing. Theirs is a legitimate and honest question. Doubtless some men by disposition cannot accept the discipline and the slowness of the middle way; others must be up and about the revolution directly and immediately. But if the result is to leave these countless little centers of Christian faith under the care of cautious Milquetoasts or to have them torn asunder by brash martyrs, we are indeed at the threshold of a dark age. The fact is that by his faithfulness to his primary task the parish minister is a critical agent of social betterment.

A layman I know who has long been concerned about racial discrimination recently chaired an interfaith committee which is trying to change the attitude and policies of a local realty board. When his committee met with members of the realty board, it found the board had no real desire even to discover if there could be any common ground. One influential member of the realty board group, it turned out, is also a Protestant layman, a member of a church whose minister is most outspoken and active in every issue for social change that comes along; but this man and his minister have never met personally. Simply with an eye to effecting social improvement, would an hour in a picket line or an hour spent establishing a relationship with that member of his congregation have been more responsible use of the minister's time?

In our church there were two young men who are brothers. One was a new graduate of a theological school, intending to take up a parish ministry eventually. In the meanwhile he was working for a year or more with the Southern Christian Leadership Conference. Before he went south his request to be ordained was fulfilled despite some objections from his pastor, who thought he should go as a layman. Some parishioners said, "I suppose it is all right for him to go. Some ministers just have to do that sort of thing." Later that winter his lawyer brother went to Mississippi to gather affidavits in the voter registration drive. A good many in the parish—especially the lawyers—said, "What goes? Maybe I should stick my neck out too."

CHAPTER 3

THE SPIRIT AND
THE STRATEGY

(Chapter 3 is the original version of an article requested by the
United Church Herald for a special issue prepared in connection with
the Eighth General Synod of the United Church of Christ, June 1971.
The four concerns selected for major consideration by the Synod
were "The Faith Crisis," "Racial Justice," "Peace and U.S. Power,"
and "The Local Church.")

Once we understand the theological and practical absurdity of listing the "local church" as one of *several* urgent concerns of the church, we will have taken a long step forward into
a renewed and promising era for the Christian religion. Immediately it must be made absolutely clear that such listing is
absurd only because the "local church" is a unique and fundamental phenomenon of Christian faith upon which everything
else is dependent. To consider such a sweeping claim seriously
it must also be clearly declared that by "local church" we do
not mean only the traditional congregation but any group of
persons who come together in the name of Jesus Christ, seeking to be open to his presence and obedient to his spirit. That
is the church. And it is always "local" in the sense that it does
not occur apart from a particular people in a particular place.
The light of that truth is arising even among Roman Catholics.

So Hans Küng declares that the local church "is in no way to be seen as a subdivision of the real 'Church.' The whole Church can only be understood in terms of the local Church and its concrete actions. The local Church is the real Church." [1] The local church then is the heart of the whole enterprise.

The local church is not faith's creation, something which men who believe in Jesus Christ may organize if they wish, like a task force or synod or ad hoc committee to implement their faith in him. It is not the *consequence* of faith; it is faith's *agency!* The Christian religion is a community affair. It is the new Israel, not a new philosophy. Faith in Jesus Christ as Lord and Savior does not arrive out of the blue. It blossoms out of the community in which he is rooted—the community of Abraham, Isaac, and Jacob; the community of Calvin, Edwards, and Gladden—and that community is sustained and corrected and continued by a book and in a tradition. That particular book and that particular tradition are the framework of that community which takes different forms, underground and overground, generation upon generation, as it gathers in his name.

That Divine Community is not made lively by doctrine formulated after the Fact by theologians, nor is it made vibrant by resolutions framed by any pope or general synod. It is made alive, awake, vibrant, powerful by Christ's promised presence where two or three gather *in his name.* If that be localism, so be it! It is a localism which has had the power to move out from Jerusalem to the whole inhabited earth and to build, criticize, dispose of, and rebuild structures and instrumentalities to enlarge Christ's power to destroy injustice and inaugurate peace.

In years past insofar as the local church was vital, deeply rooted in biblical presuppositions about God and man, when it was faithfully alert and open to God's revelation in Christ, when public worship was both inner experience and outward witness, tremendous energy was released for tremendous enterprise! What an exciting record it is: "foreign" missions, Christian higher education, church union, world peace, racial justice. Today those tremendous enterprises remain! Their urgency is the urgency of their logical consequences, and their logical consequences are in the urgency of any concern for race and peace. Alas, those tremendous enterprises do indeed remain, *but* the specifically Christian energy to implement them is waning. Yet, in a day when peace is no longer a cultural luxury but an international necessity, we do not have the funds to send abroad even the pitifully few able missionaries of the Lord ready to go. The same situation prevails in other areas of Christian mission: race, education, ecumenism—the rightful concerns of all Christians and all churches. Where have all the resources gone, the money, the enthusiasm, the gladness?

I am reminded of a bit of doggerel:

> There was a dachshund,
> Once so long
> He hadn't any notion
> How long it took to notify
> His tail of his emotion;
> And so it happened, while his eyes
> Were filled with woe and sadness,
> His little tail went wagging on
> Because of previous gladness.[2]

Well, that tail is slowing down, and before it is too late Christians must recognize that the previous gladness cannot sustain present enterprise much longer. The woe and sadness, the something amiss, are in the local church. To harangue against it and simultaneously plead with it for funds is a curiously irrational response to the profound sadness afflicting it, a sadness, a leanness of spirit, a weakness of strategy which must be the single, overwhelming, practical and theological concern of the churches and their leaders for the next few years.

46

If some lovely, new gladness is to fill the local church and keep the whole body, tail and all, wagging, help is needed at two major dimensions of its life. These may be defined as "inner" and "outer" or, more broadly and practically, as the dimension of "the spirit" and the dimension of "the strategy."

THE SPIRIT

In regard to the spirit, is there more serious judgment upon our "middle-class" religion than that brought by our own young people? From the rise of the drug cult in suburbia to the renewed popularity of such charming but limited religious poets as Kahlil Gibran and William Blake, our youth are crying out for that which deals with the inner reality of human existence. We have thought all they wanted was social action; and *that* they still want and demand most urgently and rightly. But many churches long on social action are still short on youth! They also want something to purge the woe and sadness of that man they see in us and fear in themselves against whom P. T. Forsyth warned our fathers. He is the man who, finding nothing *within* him which is *over* him, succumbs to that which is *around* him!

In the absence of a spiritual life with any vigor to it in the churches, our youth are hunting it elsewhere and coming up with the weirdest assortment of spiritual wares. One "churchly" group living together near my home looks and behaves like a senior Pilgrim Fellowship of 1950. But they follow an Oriental leader, and when they put on a Creation Dance it is straight from Genesis but *without* the serpent and the expulsion! Such is the mishmash of which Margaret Mead warns as our youth build a religion without disciplined access to the "liturgy, poetry, imagery of the historical church."

As we endeavor to point out in this book, we are children of an age that has come to a dead end. It is an age which has drummed into us from earliest childhood that the only adequate and trustworthy categories of experience are the rational, the objective, the demonstrable, the provable. The spiritual sadness of a church nurtured on these philosophical dogmas is evident in the deadliness of the majority of our congregations when they are at worship—that is, at the center of their lives. With such dogmas we do better in adult study groups, although you should try to promote them in the shadow of a great university to see how foolish the church can look when it tries to disguise itself as a school.

Such concern with the spirit, with the inner life of the church, is no escape from the implications of its life in the world. Twice in recent years I have been morally certain of the moving of the Holy Spirit in the midst of an ordinary, local church meeting. In both instances a diverse congregation was led with substantial energy and unity to elect the higher risk of two proposals before it. One such decision took that local church into deep personal and financial involvement in the urban-racial crisis; the other decision led it with surprise and delight into uncovering new styles of parish life for a new age. Both decisions were accompanied by a sense of inner revival of the church as a body.

THE STRATEGY OR "OUT, DAMN COMMA"

The second major dimension where help is needed in the life of the local church is the dimension of strategy. It all hangs on the presence or the absence of a comma. In Ephesians 4:11–12 we read: "And his gifts were that some should be apostles, some prophets, some evangelists, some pastors and teachers, for the equipment of the saints, for the work of ministry, for building up the body of Christ."

This familiar rendering with the comma after "saints" assumes that the work of ministry is the function of a special ecclesiastical office. In a recent study of this passage C. S. Cowles writes that such an assumption, buttressed as it is "by centuries of tradition, represents a misunderstanding of the New Testament. . . . More than that, it paralyzes and constricts the mission of the Church in the world. It emasculates the greatest potential for service which the Church has: the laity." [3] Well, I should say so! Cowles adds that Markus Barth claims that "no passage in the Bible is more crucial than this for the welfare and mission of the Christian Church today." [4]

The crucial comma is the one after "saints." Leave it in and you have the basis for a passive laity. Remove it, as many scholars claim the context and grammar demand, and you have the basis for an active laity in no wise passive or subordinate to the clergy. This reaffirmation of the "priesthood of all believers" is hopeful and surprising when we encounter it, as we do, in the documents of Vatican II. But it should surprise no member of the Protestant churches, children as we are of the Reformation. Yet, the truth remains that, as in other matters, while Rome moves to correct its distortions of biblical religion, we move to embrace them.

There are countless congregations who view the church's ministry as that work done by the minister. But worse! there are countless ministers who so see their role and bypass their stiff-necked congregations, so slow of heart are they to believe and to act. In so doing they neglect their chief duty under New Testament strategy, namely, to equip the saints (all the members of the church) for the work of ministry, to help them to be prepared as Christ's men and women in the magnificently strategic places they occupy "scattered abroad within the structures of the world."

As denominations, we must resolutely turn from a similar fundamental mistake in understanding the function of our national boards and regional bodies. Many of these are now commonly referred to as "instrumentalities." Besides being an impossibly gross word as far as the English language is concerned, it reflects a dangerous and deadly tendency to see the ministry of the church in the world (for example in matters of peace and race) as something to be "instrumented" by these bodies.

Now, to be sure, there are crucial and churchly tasks which can be done most effectively only by such larger bodies. Much of the most conspicuous part of the prophetic task of the church in our day must be borne by the elected and recognized national and state officers and the boards and councils of the church. The vast opportunity and difficult requirements of the mass media require centralization of expertise and financial resources for wise expenditure of the limited means of a church so rich in money and so poor in available funds as mainline Protestantism in the U.S.A. But these necessities have led to an elitism in denominational and ecumenical structures quite as limiting as a ministerial elitism in the local church. That horrendous comma in Ephesians which Luther helped exorcise has been welcomed back with open arms by Christians eager to have the church's ministry fulfilled by professional clergy or delegated to a distant board.

"Out, damn comma, out!" Consider the empowerment of the whole church, of all its boards and institutions and missions at home and throughout the world, in all its ghettos and Ghanas, if all the professional clergy and the denominational instrumentalities turned their considerable energies and talents and resources toward awakening and equipping "the saints," the local church, for the work of ministry in the world. There is a new world aborning—or should we say "agreeing"—and the old-style local church of organizational man, passive and delegating, is inadequate to that day. Yet, the essence of that local church is desperately needed by that world now in travail and rebirth. In their poverty of spirit and impotence of strategy many local churches are announcing that they are running out of gladness and can't wag their tails any longer. Is there no ministry

50

of empowerment for them from both professional clergy and "higher bodies" of the church?

What practical measures can Christians propose which would help to bring about this radical reorientation of denominational priority and would place us in the forefront of church renewal and refreshment of the fabric of modern society? There are many suggestions which come to mind. Some may not fall within our immediate grasp, others may be totally and recklessly impossible, and all are futile if they do not help local churches become places marked by joy and gladness and wide open to many life styles. I submit a few in the hope of stimulating others and provoking some clear, concrete, dramatic action.

1. Declare a state of emergency in the church and direct the raising of millions of dollars or reappropriation of other funds to launch a crash program for renewal of the local church. Such a program might include:

    a. A fund to facilitate the early retirement of local ministers over fifty or sixty years of age who are grimly hanging on to a pastorate primarily out of economic necessity.

    b. A fund to help ministers under fifty or sixty years of age who do not really wish to remain in the ministry to get established in another vocation.

    c. A plan to design and widely advertise among the *laymen* of the local church a program for the re-education of the present committed clergyman, especially refreshing him for his much neglected primary task as theologian in the community of faith. Encourage conference ministers and bishops to raise serious questions with the officers of any local church which does not provide the opportunity, apart from vacation time, for its minister's professional refreshment.

d. Ways to speed the enlistment and preparation of new men and women for the professional ministry to fill the many positions opened by releasing the disillusioned and the defeated.

2. Stimulate and encourage with funds a program directed by a theological faculty which would not recommend a student to a church or a church to a student unless both were willing to participate for a year in a parish renewal program. A three-way partnership would be formed for a wonderful year of growth: congregation, seminary, and new minister. Each would learn from the others and many potential disasters could be made instruments of learning for all members of the partnership.

3. Insist upon examination of the credentials of every nominee for the boards of the church and for executive officers. What has been his or her experience in the local church either as lay member or minister, underground or overground? How has this person responded to the conflict which characterizes many parishes today? Has he or she been effective in broadening and deepening the involvement of the local church in the crises of the nation and of the world? Is this person's appearance on the national scene a matter of fleeing the local church or helping to renew it?

4. Establish extensive schools of parish management in every part of the nation for laity and clergy modeled after similar schools conducted through the National Council of Churches for church administrative officers. Such schools would seek to teach practical skills in leadership of meetings and in creative handling of tension, resistance, and conflict.

5. Take action to increase "participatory priesthood" in the local church by having the percentage allocation of church funds determined by the local congregation. The ensuing administrative hassle for the various instrumentalities might be well worthwhile in terms of education and partici-

pation on both sides and the subsequent increase in support by the local congregation. The competition fostered could be healthy for all levels of the church.

"And what more shall I say? For time would fail me" . . . and you! Undoubtedly, many of these suggestions may reflect in part some ongoing program or concern somewhere in our churches. Many of them have strong support in places both high and low. All this will be too little too late, however, if we seek to meet the crisis of the church, which is fundamentally the crisis of the local church, with anything less than the boldest and most costly leadership.

It is not a matter of one claim competing with another. It is a prelude to disaster if the various partisan demands of the churches so overwhelm and distress and divide us that we fail to take stunningly faithful and adventurous action on this one overwhelmingly central problem. If this claim is put aside or met halfheartedly, then ultimately all other claims come down with it.

All these strategies and more must be tried, but they may skirt the basic issue, the religious issue, the source of excitement and conviction and ardor about Jesus Christ. How helpless we are at the center of our poverty—the absence of gladness in faith! It is easier to sketch church strategy than it is to be open to the recovery of the Spirit. We have some great local churches but they are seldom conspicuous. They are great because the people who gather there are touched again and again by God and are constantly restored and healed and forgiven. They are changed. They are filled with joy and gladness—and with power! "Power to the People!" Yes, to people who have met in the name of Jesus Christ and who seek to be open to his presence and obedient to his spirit— so how crucial is the quality of our localism!

"Therefore lift your drooping hands and strengthen your weak knees. . . . Strive for peace with all men, and for the holiness without which no one will see the Lord. See to it that no one fail to obtain the grace of God; that no 'root of bitterness' spring up and cause trouble (Heb. 12:12, 14–15)."

CHAPTER 4

LIVING IN STYLE: REPORT FROM A PARISH CHURCH

At half past eight on a Sunday morning in January eleven men and women stood around the communion table in the chapel of First Congregational Church of Berkeley, participating in the sacrament of the Lord's Supper. A quarter hour later all the church buildings were astir with what might seem an unlikely assortment of activities. Choir rehearsal, a class on Isaiah, an early activities program for children, and even a coffeehouse open for business surprised no one; but other sights were unexpected. Kitchen cabinets and denim vests were being set out for display by craftsmen and seamstresses from black-owned and operated Ghettos, Inc., while deaconesses arranged an exhibit showing some of their ways of dealing with urban loneliness among the elderly. Upstairs were counselors from a runaway center, spreading out informational leaflets; down the street, just beyond the nursery school playground, young people were opening the youth house for visitors.

This was "Inside-Out Sunday," an effort at bridging the gap between people inside the church and people outside the church, an opening out and inviting in for exposure and understanding and mutual enrichment. At ten o'clock people came to worship, bringing guests. Neighbors, friends, associates were invited, students and university administrators, civic officials and urban project personnel. Then, for two hours following the service, people visited exhibits and demonstrations, talked with project workers, inquired, commented, responded. The intent was to show people outside the church something of the nature and scope of the life of a present-day Protestant parish, something of the streams which feed into and flow from that corporate worship which is the pulsing heart of the church. In keeping with this purpose the varied exhibits represented the internal life of the church (the gathered church), its outreach in the local community and beyond (the church dispersed), and the groups which it hosts in its buildings (the church interacting).

Most significant among the displays was the lively mural encircling the walls of the assembly hall, for this was the report of the congregation to itself on its own deliberate search for a life style for the 70's. A running line wove in and out among the paintings, posters, poetry, and photos: "worship the living God" . . . "take part joyously" . . . "trust each other" . . . "perspective and humor" . . . "people of all ages" . . . "differences can be beautiful" . . . "tell the Good News joyfully." This was the exuberant, pictorial progress report on a process initiated almost a year earlier, in the first months of the new decade.

That decade had opened against a background of increasing tensions and periodic crises—national and local, civic, academic and churchly—which threatened to make crisis-dealing a way of life. It was clearly time for reflection, introspection, and projection, and to this task the long-range planning board of the church applied itself with vigor. Ten years earlier, at a time of change of pastorate, the church had carried out a careful self-study, "Patterns for Progress." The plan for that study, reflected in its title, was appropriate and useful in 1960. The "patterns" had served their purpose, but it would not do now to attempt to define specific objectives for each area of church responsibility and concern. This year the pressing questions were of a different sort. They were about the church and its people, about a purpose in being and a manner of living. We needed to look at unity and diversity at conviction and conflict, at humility, honesty, and humor. Indeed, we needed to inquire into our being as a church, searching out the whether and why and how of uniting in the name and spirit of Jesus Christ.

Procedure could be effective only if it faithfully reflected this intent. So the board determined to devise ways of helping the congregation to engage in discovering and developing a valid and recognizable style for its life as a church. The differences which pressed on us were acknowledged as real. The unfolding of the process was to be left honestly open, even though this might lead us to become several partially or wholly separate congregations. Such was the calculated risk. Would we find diversity to be cause for division or might it be discovered as a source of strength and a reason for rejoicing?

The board realized that it had a monumental task. The discovery process must be imaginative to draw maximum involvement, including extensive participation by youth. Small discussion groups would be of crucial importance. The process must have form but remain sufficiently flexible to allow us to grow and move with it. The board felt its way slowly. As a first step, members of the church and its boards and committees were encouraged to list problems and ideas to be considered in the 70's. Material submitted covered so much territory that the subcommittee never could organize it adequately! The board then searched for a fresh way of inviting people to come together on the basis of similarity of approach to life. After many a lively debate, the method chosen was at least as contemporary as the computer. Members and friends of the church would be invited to take the Rokeach Value Survey in which each participant arranges, in order of importance to him, a series of eighteen "end values," such as wisdom, salvation, true friendship, and eighteen "means values," such as honest, forgiving, obedient.[1] Computer analysis of the data would be programmed to list the respondents in four divisions on the basis of maximum similarity of expressed value system. Such divisions would be too broad to have great intrinsic significance, but, in Peter Berger's terminology, it would be *plausible* to expect that persons so grouped might talk profitably together. Further subdivision of the four sections could be by time convenience for the participants.

Now the process took shape. We would form four sections and each section would attempt to design a model for its church life in respect to four major areas: worship, Christian growth, outreach, and life together. We would then assemble at a weekend retreat to present the models, hopefully in some dramatic form, respond to them, play, worship, and ask where the process pointed. PACT was born: *P*lay the value game, *A*ttend your plausibility group, *C*elebrate at Asilomar, *T*ake off for the 80's.

PACT was launched. Copies of the value survey with an invitation to participate were mailed to members and closely associated friends of the church. There were approximately 800 returns. Conversation in cloister and coffeehouse assumed fresh content: "I put 'clean' low on my list. So why am I offended by untidy, dirty people on the street?" "What do you think salvation means in a value scheme?" Data were assembled and a computer programmed. Our experts posted printouts on the assembly walls, showing value system profiles for the church and for each of four sections. People rushed to read the lists and laughed or complained or wondered. "How could you and I possibly be together?" We also met each other slipping into the library to do a bit of hasty reference work on section names: Horace Bushnell, Jonathan Edwards, Washington Gladden, Henry Ward Beecher. One telephone message came in: "Please tell Mr. Bushnell I cannot be there for the meetings."

Next came the invitation to take part in discussion groups which would meet once a week for four weeks. Each section offered groups meeting daytimes and evenings, weekdays and Sundays. As sign-ups increased we grew to twenty groups in all, incorporating almost 400 people. Group leaders and recorders were enlisted in advance on the basis of special skills. Four couples, one for each section, accepted responsibility for coordinating the groups and for guiding the sections in assembling and presenting their reports. These forty-eight persons were prepared for their specific tasks through sessions with a wise process trainer, a member of the planning board fully conversant with the purpose of the groups. Theological base for the topic each week was given in the Sunday sermons, the cruciality of this base being set forth in the minister's announcement of the series:

All of our discussion about the church in the seventies may be vain babbling if we do not invite the Lord of the Church to be present. He comes when we seriously talk about him. That is the essence of Christian conversation. So the sermons are planned to set forth in plain English some of the important and basic truths about Him—Him and us. The first sermon will be an Easter sermon because that is where the Church really began and so it is where we should start. Then we move backwards over the remembered events and teachings of that Palestinian man. That is the way the first Christians did. That is the way the Scripture is written. So we come to a Christmas sermon on Easter Day.[2]

Ministers did not take part in the groups, not wanting to risk inhibiting or influencing discussion. Most groups had a good age spread. Some proceeded through four weeks with high enthusiasm, most retained active interest, a few dwindled, none dissolved. Meanwhile, interest in the coming Asilomar retreat grew and with it the need to finance the affair in some way that would equalize the load and insure that no one would be kept away by cost. Hence, a great "attic-to-basement" sale was held, with some new, firm friendships formed in the process.

The Asilomar event was a church family occasion with possibly as many as three quarters of the regularly active members taking part, again almost 400 participants—men and women, youth and babes. Apprehensions of the planning committee and uneasiness of the uninitiated subsided as we came together for an opening session in the rustic beach lodge. Beribboned poles identified the Bushnell, Edwards, Gladden, and Beecher sections, stirring both lighthearted banter and serious interest. Yards of butcher-paper graffiti space and slit-top boxes with handy notepads invited spontaneous response to anything said, done, or omitted and solicited questions for further probing. All such bits of paper were carefully saved, read, and reported.

The conference proceeded with dramatized reports and talking time, meals shared, and recreation which ranged in choice from bird walks to ball games. Square dancing after the evening session was another great age-mixer, youth graciously forming squares with their elders, and some old-timers outswinging their grandchildren to the final call. Communion was celebrated on the beach in the early morning, and before noon we held our Sunday service in the round, drawing together the threads of emotion and thought, the needs revealed, the dreams dreamed, and the hopes roused.

Such was the form. The outcome was discovery. Something had been astir beginning with response to the value survey and the surprising participation in the plausibility group discussions. Of course, no group could be expected to bring forth a full characterization of its "church for the 70's" from four ninety-minute sessions, yet the written reports and dramatized presentations did raise important questions and introduce provocative ideas. There were indeed even some slight, recognizable differences between the four sections. Clearly, however, the significance of this exercise was not to be found in words and ideas, important as these were, and it was fortunate that the board had protected the freedom of the process by declining to project the nature of the culminating session. The significant discovery came at a meeting late on Saturday night. The reports had not yielded descriptions of a life style or styles definable in words, but they had most surely brought a church style to conscious life and given it fresh momentum. Culmination could not be a summary; it would only be a moment of recognition and a time of undergirding of the ongoing process.

This was accomplished in an open response session with no invited speakers or primed questioners, an admittedly risky procedure. Some contributions were constructive, others highly critical. Speakers grew increasingly forthright as the hour progressed, with scribes recording each item visibly on long scrolls on the stage. The value of the session increased correspondingly and the meeting closed with much material in front of us for further exploration. Recognition of the essential continuity of the process came in capsule form when someone said: "It's all well and good for us to have expressed these areas of difference and still found we could have fun together, but now let's *deal* with the conflicts." It came again when another asked: "How shall we incorporate those who are not here in what has happened to us?"

Indeed, how can we share with other churches the values which have emerged for us from this process? There is nothing earthshaking to report, yet our enrichment has been great. As the process of discovery continues, we are learning more about dealing with problems instead of dreading them; we are wakening to the possibility of facing conflict more in faith

61

than in fear; we are coming to know one another better and to trust one another more, to take useful risks, to welcome joy, to live in love. Of course, there is pain in the growing— growing pains. So our report to our sister churches may best be given through glimpses of the continuing process, the *T* of PACT as we have taken off for the 80's.

Worship is the keystone. "Reality," "involvement," and "fulfillment" were dominant words in the discussions of worship, and these needs were addressed in planning the services for the retreat. They influence our present forms of worship. A brief weekly service of communion served by various ordained members of the congregation meets a need for a few early-risers. Other persons who wanted an informal, free-form service were invited to take leadership in arranging occasions for worship for Sunday afternoons. Group planning fell by the wayside, and the "church professionals," with an uncommitted committee, tried to respond to the request with a variety of five o'clock events hopefully attractive to almost anyone—students, families with children, and all the folk who wanted novelty and action in their celebration of the Lord. Folk singer and rock band, organ concert and scripture storytelling provided occasions of varying attraction, but we soon recognized that most of this programming rose from no overflowing hearts and led to no fulfillment. A need remained and again interested persons were invited to take counsel. This time a few concerned laymen presented a new proposal. They wanted worship rather than entertainment, participation rather than performance, informality rather than formlessness. A half dozen families with small children and another half dozen persons of assorted ages began to gather by the fireside in the church lounge each Sunday afternoon. They gradually developed a ritual, learning their chosen songs and responses, expressing their own prayers. Planning and leadership were shared in rotation. This form also changed in time. It seemed good to the group to come together monthly rather than weekly but to extend these occasions to include the sharing of an informal meal. Need for more adult conversation and reflection led to monthly midweek meetings for study and planning. So the pattern continues to evolve to meet the need. This group, faithful to the intention of Christian worship and free to find its own forms and rituals, is serving a number of persons who find themselves unable to participate wholeheartedly in the larger corporate experience of the church. For most persons involved, however, this coming together is in addition to rather than in place of the primary church service.

That central service of corporate worship has also been refreshed. We sense a heightened expectation in our worshiping and perhaps have some glimmer of awareness of being a people engaged in a vital act together. Attendance has increased slowly. New young people appear in the choir and on the ushering teams, instrumentalists offer their music, the lay moderator presents the parish notices. Praise and prayer reach out in less obvious ways as well. A few more people are aware of the quiet work of the prayer fellowship and make their requests for intercession or thanksgiving. More students and passersby come into the chapel to meditate, occasionally leaving messages in response to the sermons and devotional materials provided for them.

The second area considered was Christian growth. Our style indicators for this decade point toward greater unity of effort along with diversity of method and a determined crossing of generation lines. The Old Testament theme for church school courses that fall provided focus and texts for a series of sermons. Weekly sermon seminars (chapter 6) stimulated reflection on the scripture as preparation for the preaching. The following year the theme of church history, accepted as a churchwide emphasis, was highlighted by four series of lectures and was developed further by the use of art and music appropriate to the early, medieval, Reformation, and contemporary periods. More can be done to bring the whole people alive to the issues of any given theme. We see a direction also in bringing children into interaction with a wider spectrum of adults and youth in their classroom experiences as well as in worship and workshops and parties. Parents of youth are meeting monthly for discussions—sometimes with the young people, sometimes separately. Several new types of adult groups have emerged. Some have developed a substantial existence and are dealing effectively with vital issues. Others are still feeling their way. Some flop. There is talk of long-weekend family-type retreats as prime time for Christian education and life exploration. Interest has been aroused in taking a long look at questions about families and sexuality and life styles. What about men and women, marriage and parenthood, home and vocation here and now? So a weekend conference at the church has been planned around the theme "Nurtured in Love." It is for old and young, single or married, conventional or liberated. Its most pressing purpose is to help us to meet one another, to hear one another, to understand one another, to appreciate one another, and to learn from one another. If it results in some decrease in fear and suspicion and some increase in trust and faith, it will have been worth all the long months of careful thought and study and preparation in which the planning board has engaged.

Style of outreach work evolves gradually and requires continuing adaptation. The touchiest points of conflict are here, the knotty questions. Outcome of the PACT considerations was the decision that we would bring the conflicts into the open and deal with them. To gloss them over is only to allow bitterness to fester. We determined that we would encourage and assist concerned persons and groups to find or establish appropriate channels for action without expecting consensus of the congregation. We would invite consideration of issues. A visitor might detect the style in seeing material offered by such groups as the Peace Brigade. He might hear a speaker reporting on a mission to Hanoi or attend a forum on issues in an agricultural workers' strike, and some Sunday morning perchance he would find the assembly hall turned into what we have dubbed "Sproul Plaza South," a place where anyone may set up a table to invite signatures on political petitions. Such a style is distinct both from that of the church as a power block and the church as uninvolved. It has validity, however, only if the expression of concerns and the address to needs is constantly nourished and informed by response to the gospel. It recognizes that reiteration of righteous moralisms and espousal of simplistic solutions honor neither God nor man.

There is a conscious quality also to what we have called our life together. It is seen predominantly in the mood described in the report as "take part joyously." A new program of time and talent stewardship aims to bring people into positions where they can serve rather than asking them to accept posts they may simply occupy. Boards enlist ad hoc task forces, thereby spreading the work load broadly. Three new lay assistant staff positions have evolved. One assistant is parish visitor and coordinator of volunteers, another is coordinator of children's work, the third serves in campus ministry. Each is a volunteer, serving on a regular basis for twelve to twenty hours a week and taking full part in weekly meetings with the ministers and the moderator. Such a lay-clergy combination has already noticeably enriched the "staff."

Other evidences of style included an all-church staff interaction session in which the moderator led secretaries, custodians, and ministers in an afternoon of role-playing and reflection which aired both anxieties and irritations, and freed relationships amazingly. Some church boards are questioning seriously how they can perform a significant ministry through their area of administration. Others may take a fresh look at the pastoral possibilities both of their tasks and of their meetings after a workshop day for all board members.

One Sunday the high school youth were talking with the minister. There was a reference to PACT and the Asilomar retreat. Someone observed, "Yes, it was fun at the time, but what good was it? Everything is just the same as before." The remark passed. Later in the evening there were comments about increased buoyancy in the church services and an easier acceptance of casual dress. A young listener challenged, "I thought you said PACT didn't make a difference!"

It seems it did and it does. This would account for even the faltering, half-reluctant, half-embarrassed step of lay evangelism involved in inviting guests to an inside-out Sunday to bridge a gap in understanding. It would account also for the boldness of offering through Pacific School of Religion a summer workshop entitled "The Local Congregation and Its Ministry," with the ministers and congregation as instructors. This was offered as a mutual discovery workshop and such it proved to be. Lay men and women of the church and ministers of assorted denominations and types of parish situation worked seriously together for three weeks of twice-weekly, four-hour sessions to our mutual edification and delight.

It is well that the *T* in PACT stood for "take off" rather than "tie up," for the outcome was a process rather than a package, a process of openness and involvement and discovery moving us to a deliberately chosen but continually evolving style of life. It was crucial, then, that we try to draw the entire congregation as deeply as possible into the experiences which had been lived out in the plausibility groups and at the retreat. This was done as we posted the photographs, sang the songs, and presented in a morning service the skit on use of conflict which had been particularly moving for the company at Asilomar. Interpretation continued through conversation and the distribution of reports. Involvement expanded further through months of questioning and discussion as the planning board struggled to delineate the style with sufficient clarity to be useful in guiding and evaluating the work of the boards and committees and the life of the church. The process proceeded as we discovered through trial and error, through tense hours and sometimes amusing aftermaths that we are fundamentally one people in Christ not four or ten or two, that we are enriched by variety and may well increase in strength through appropriate use of conflict.

Our particular style indicators are simply our report to ourselves like a set of words which have determinative value in a family but lose their concrete, specific content in the outside world. These words have now become our private symbols, filled with living meanings. Another church would find its own symbols, filled with its own discoveries. Indeed, even the discovery process itself cannot be transposed directly. Discovery implies uniqueness. Exploration, whatever form it takes, must have a quality of venture to it best approached in a high-spirited mood. The explorer's kit will include a receptivity alike to pain and joy, a large measure of faith, and a wide-awake imagination. For what is imagination to a man of faith but openness to the Holy Spirit, free-moving and unlimited?

So to our sister churches, joy!

CHAPTER 5

POP SERMONS

If anyone were to put a stopwatch on the various emphases in mainline Protestantism, he would discover that even as the pulpit and the table ordinarily dominate our *place* of worship, so the sermon dominates our *time* of worship. There it is with all its bulk and prominence: an inescapable focal point, an irrepressible symbol in our time of worship. A great many Protestants, regarding the sermon time spot as a wordy void, have moved toward other forms, with the pulpit retired to one side and the sermon cut down to a few paragraphs.

This antisermon movement is indeed threatening to one whose vocation is tied to the pulpit, but the truth might as well be faced: the sermon has come upon bad days! Some argue that its slippage is largely due to the revolution in communication—radio and television and all that sort of thing. So it may be, but I believe that what we are faced with is the result of a decay in sermons themselves, a decay which preceded and quickened their decline.

TO BE MOVED, NOT JUST INFORMED

Justus George Lawler, who is a professor of theology and literature at St. Xavier College in Chicago and editor of a distinguished Roman Catholic quarterly, has delivered a scathing denunciation of the so-called God-is-dead theology, suggesting that it should be called "pop theology." Regarding pop art he writes: "Since pop painting was so negligible as to be almost non-existent as an artifact (Painting is dead!), all that really mattered to a truly contemporary critic was talk about, around, behind, and across the picture."[1] As I read that I thought about the reactions from the pew to many sermons, and I began to wonder if our problem is not that what we have today are "pop sermons." As I explored Professor Lawler's essay more deeply, I found some light beginning to shine on the two sides of the sermon problem: the side which rests in the pew and the side which rests in the pulpit.

Professor Lawler mentions the contemporary art critic. Well, there are plenty of contemporary sermon critics, and we must remember that critics both praise and condemn. Lawler claims that pop art was so negligible as an artifact, as a product of human workmanship, that all that remained for the critic was to talk about, around, behind, and across it. He suggests that men could not be moved by such art, so they discussed it.

A symptom of similar decay in the sermon shows itself, I believe, in the breaking out all across American Protestantism of what are called "talk-back sessions." When the sermon is over and the worship is concluded, people are invited to engage in a discussion of the sermon. The preacher, presumably removed from the protection of the pulpit, is asked to explain, answer, "enter into dialogue" with, the people. This would be splendid if the sermon were intended as a lecture to educate the people, if it were meant as direct advice upon which men of goodwill might disagree, or even if it were offered to increase one's understanding of some theological proposition. Now the sermon may legitimately do any one or all these things. But if that is *all* it can manage, if that is its reason for being, it scarcely deserves more time than scripture or prayer, and a lecture hall would be a more suitable environment for its delivery.

But in Protestant worship the sermon is offered to move men, not to educate them; to touch them at the springs of their being, not just to proffer them advice or counsel. For that there are more able experts elsewhere. The act of preaching demands quite as much of the pew as of the pulpit in preparation and eagerness and earnest participation. It is an instrument prepared by the congregation as a community of Christian discourse—set down in the context of its history and its hope, its hymns, its prayers, its scripture. It is an instrument by which the great hand of the Eternal grasps us, people and preacher alike; a hand which leads or drives us out to the periphery of life where we get a sense of the "mystery that there is a world" at all and not just nothing; a hand which shakes us out of complacency and knocks the carefully nurtured dust off our ease; a hand which opens us up with that Word which is sharper than any two-edged sword. In that opening the healing which is in God's love begins, and our sorrow can be turned to joy, our fear to hope, and our misery to the ecstasy of those who know that nothing can separate them from his love! The sermon, properly conceived and properly received, is far more than a religious address; it is an instrument which anchors us in that which is beyond us and reveals that "the light we see is the Light by which we see."

When that happens life is changed, renewed, refreshed; fears are banished and hopes refurbished; guilt is swept away. And when that does happen, who in heaven's name is then ready to go off into a room somewhere and analyze the instrument of his renewal! It is as though after a high moment of holy communion it were prescribed that we should go to the kitchen and discuss what kind of bread was used and why.

ANTICIPATION: THE PREREQUISITE

The decay of the pulpit is inevitable when congregation and preacher alike never expect or prepare to be moved to repentance and to the amendment of life, never look up eagerly for some break in their darkness, no longer anticipate that the text "faith comes from what is heard" may be true. So a gentleman writes indignantly to *Life* magazine after a series titled "Churches Take a Cue from Show Biz" has appeared: "Has it ever occurred to the churches that our contempt of them arises out of their persistent habit of adapting the Divine to our needs, and that . . . we might like to be struck down by an inaccessible Mystery beyond any grasp?"

This does not mean that the implications of sermons should not be discussed any more than it means that the implications of holy communion should not be lived out, incorporated into our total life style. Every congregation worth its salt is working in these days on means and methods of providing more and better opportunities to reason together about the implications of faith and how to implement it in our society. The church must be in the world and for the world, the servant of the world. But all that is vain and without direction or motivation if the Divine be kept hidden and if congregational renewal and personal commitment be always postponed.

So an Orthodox priest, speaking at a Notre Dame conference on Vatican II, addressed a question to the Catholic Church which may quite as well be addressed to all of us who are so preoccupied with determination to make Christ "relevant" to secular man that it begins to seem as though it is Christ who must conform. Fr. John Meyendorff asked if the "Roman Church [is] always right in its traditional preoccupation . . . to find solutions to all human problems, to

71

guide, to feed, to advise, to rule and to direct instead of *showing*." It is this "showing forth" to which the proper sermon is devoted; it is this for which the pew must be expectant and prepared and ready to receive. For as has been said, "Faith comes from what is heard, and what is heard comes by the preaching of Christ."

But alas, that brings us to the other side of the problem of the sermon: the pulpit. How can such expectations be demanded of the pew when those who sit there have waited so long and with such disappointment?

Another sentence of Professor Lawler's about pop art bears home on the pulpit. Here we must remember that the critic is in the pulpit as well as in the pew, and that it is that critic who chooses themes as well as illustrations, who sorts over ideas as well as adjectives. Professor Lawler could well be writing of the preacher himself: "Pop art made the critic more important than the artwork itself, even as pop theology makes the concepts of theologians more important than the being of God." [2] Then he really takes off after one of the God-is-dead theologians: "For tangential theological discourse going off aimlessly about himself and about his ideas and his feelings and his opinions one must heed the voice of Professor ————." [3] Well, we do not need to supply that name. Every preacher needs only to remember how often his own name would fit there perfectly, for this is what the people have heard: his ideas, his feelings, his opinions. There is little faith prompted in the hearer by such human recital.

This is not so much to find fault with contemporary preachers and contemporary theological education as it is to reveal how far the so-called acids of modernity have eaten into the fabric of Protestant worship, how greatly they have corroded our confidence in God as an immediate and pressing reality. The preference for secondhand experience is the preference of the age, and the rebellion of our youth is in part a demand for the firsthand, an exposure of our timidity and our spectator complex. So the sermon is sprinkled with qualifiers—"perhaps," "it seems to me"—and the substance of the message is always tackled at the secondary level. Like pop art, the production itself is so trivial that we can only discuss it, not experience its substance.

WHEN THE "GOOD WORD" IS HEARD

The sermon which is not prepared by the preacher as well as anticipated by the people in the expectation that God can and will use our discourse to reveal himself is no sermon at all. But a sermon so prepared and received by the whole community of Christian discourse, people and preacher too, is no anachronism, no relic of a day long since passed. It stands dominant, central to our instant needs as modern men no matter where the pulpit stands. So a Protestant theologian, Albert Outler, addresses a generation confused by solemn announcements of God's death: "Now the reality of God becomes the central issue once more . . . [and the obvious task of the new generation is] to convince men of the reality of God [of his presence and grace] in a world come of age and gone to pot."

Years ago it was a custom to place a large gold coin beneath the mainmast of old sailing vessels; thus it was that even a wreck had value to those who knew. So it may be with the poorest sermon if the preacher will always try to put in, as the old Scots said, a "good word for Jesus Christ." But that word is not put in for the new generation by throwing around pious religious lingo, theological and pulpit currency long since worse off than the English pound. That good word will be spoken as Christ is heard in the dependability of nature's unfolding and in the wonder of the evolutionary process. It will be spoken as Christ's redemptive power, freeing men to love and to work, is seen in the labor of everyone—psychiatrist and physicist, teacher and grandparent—who enables and sets free, who brings order out of chaos. It will be spoken as Christ's voice is heard in the daily witness of the whole church, pulpit and pew alike, as it experiences the forgiveness he supplies and exercises the citizenship he directs. All this is what it means "to say a good word for Jesus Christ," this is what it means to preach him. If the preacher does that, then an expectant congregation will not be frustrated and disappointed. And even as the sermon goes aground on the rocks of the preacher's inevitable human limitations, some faithful soul will know to look beneath the mainmast and, with the gold coin rescued from the wreck and held aloft and shared, the preaching will go on.

So "faith comes from what is heard and what is heard comes by the preaching of Christ."

CHAPTER 6

SERMON SEMINAR

There were perhaps a dozen of them sitting around a couple of cafeteria-type folding tables in the catacomb-like cool of the basement social room of a city church. They were eating box lunches of the sort you get on some airlines with the cheapest tourist fares. They were talking about how hot it was for San Francisco even on a September day at noon. They had come from commanding concerns about price juggling and fringe benefits and legal briefs, from insistent telephones and shiny water coolers and office bets on the afternoon's game. Another sermon seminar was under way, called together on the premise that the whole church must submit itself to the discipline of the words in the Bible, waiting to hear in those words and through them the Word the living God has for His living people.

Such was the opening of a sermon in First Congregational Church of Berkeley, where members of the congregation are encouraged to engage in regular discussion with the minister in response to the text for the sermon of the coming Sunday. This discipline has become a vital part of the preacher's background work preliminary to sermon-writing. It has become an equally vital part of the preparation of the participating laymen to hear the Word as it comes to them through scripture and sermon. It is thus a means of implementing the Reformed teaching that the whole people of God are called to read, study, and respond to the scriptures.[1] Though the writing of the sermon remains the minister's task alone, his soundings of the text are amplified as parishioners share what the passage evokes for them. This is not to say that theology arises from experience, but that it is only in experience that theology can be properly grasped.

The sermon seminar at First Congregational came into being through the coalescence of several elements—the deacons' interest in prayer cells, Christian education plans for Bible study groups, the desire of the ministers to participate with others in a community of persons committed to sustain one another in a discipline of study, devotion, and service. An invitation was extended to the congregation: "Anyone who is interested in discussing the problems of faith and of life and in joining others in prayer is invited to meet with the ministers in the reception room from 8:30 to 9:30 P.M. on Wednesday. This is not another activity to support."

We were men and women of assorted ages, occupations, and interests who came that first night, seeking something, wondering about the offer. No recipe had been formulated, but the ingredients were set out for us: Bible study with both a critical and an experiential bent, an occasion to be free and frank about personal questions of life and faith, shared prayer which would be specific for the members of the group as well as for the world at large. No commitment was asked but we were invited to return each week, and the minister promised to give this meeting hour a prior claim on his time. Gradually a group took form and a pattern developed. The passage for study each week was to be the text for the following Sunday's sermon. Members of the group might prepare for the meetings by reading commentaries and by bringing with them various translations of the Bible, plus their own questions, ideas, and personal needs. All were urged to reflect on the passage in advance of the meeting.

EXPLORATIONS, QUESTIONS, PRAYER

Each session of the seminar is led by the minister who is to preach on the following Sunday. Customarily the preacher introduces the text by sketching the historical and contextual situation, then gives just enough simple exegesis to indicate where the crucial problems lie and to guard against gross misreading. He may direct attention to the existential setting for the sermon, to its place in the Christian year, or to some pressing concern in the life of the community or the parish. Sometimes he concludes by proposing a question designed to focus the discussion on a specific area or to initiate the process of free association. From this point on the minister remains, for the most part, a silent listener, taking notes on the responses which are offered. Occasionally need may arise to recall the group to its task or to help people let the text question them more deeply, but as a usual thing these functions are discharged by the participants themselves.

Questions relating to composition, leadership, and procedure for the discussion units have been resolved largely through experimentation and evaluation by the entire group. In fact, within a few months, involvement of the regular members became such that they resented any hint of tampering or of one-sided decision by the clergy—a healthy sign, but one that posed some problems. We decided to forego such advantages as might come from continuity in the small round-table groups in order to protect the basic unity of the seminar and its openness to newcomers: "counting off" brought us into different groupings week by week. We experimented with having one minister present in each group as a participant-helper, and again with assigning to each unit a lay leader selected in advance. Sometimes the groups were left to appoint their own leadership or to proceed in any way they saw fit. The "preaching" minister of the week usually circulated among the units but tried to stay on the fringe, listening.

Group procedure has altered several times in the years since the seminar started, but the period of prayer remains the keystone of the experience. It may be introduced by a rereading of the text or some related scripture. There is time for silence and for invitation to speak, often encouraged by use of the "circle" form of prayer. As prayers are voiced, each participant is asked to hold before God the persons on his right and on his left. The prayer then reaches out beyond those gathered to all whose claim is on us; it becomes universal in the prayer of Jesus, binding us together at a deeper level and at the same time releasing us and sending us forth. This quarter hour adds a dimension which keeps the seminar from fostering an unhealthy introversion.

The process was referred to in a recent sermon:

At the close we prayed together . . . and we prayed for one another; how else shall our deepest mutuality be supplied and what deeper honor do we confer than to pray for one another? We asked then that we might return to the busy places whence we had come more aware of God, more aware of life. It was a prayer that he might come as he had promised, in the midst of life. Then we each one went his separate way.

The seminar has attracted persons active in the mission of the church and in the life of the community; some are professional people, some housewives, others retired persons. It has drawn people who labor under peculiar personal stresses; others who simply seek help in hearing the Word in the scriptures. Inevitably, differences in motivation and need have led to conflicting pressures within the group. A sincere effort has been made to hold in balance the intellectual, devotional, and therapeutic interests which are demonstrated.

LIVES ARE ENRICHED

Participation decreased during the third year. Though the meetings continued to serve an important support function, creativity dropped to a point which warned of inner sterility. Hence, it was decided that the seminar would "take to the road" for a season, with the time and place of meeting to be changed every four weeks. The first series was scheduled in San Francisco at the lunch hour, a time which had proved propitious for men's round-table discussions on ethics the preceding year. The next series was scheduled for midmornings in a Berkeley home. Because most of the men were prevented by their work from attending daytime gatherings, they arranged to meet whenever they and the ministers could get together. Meanwhile, the seminar moved on, convening in downtown Berkeley or in Oakland, in homes, at the university faculty club or at the church. Such roving life obviously entails a certain loss, but it has enlarged the scope of interest and has enabled the ministers to hear what the scripture suggests to men and women of various occupations when they stop for an hour in the middle of a workday to read and to respond. Most recently, the seminar was held under the heading "Tower Time," a series of late-evening sessions set apart for the "under thirty" folk with their pastor. Sprawled on the carpet of a brick room high in the churchtower across from a university dormitory complex, students and young employed persons probed their experience of life in encounter with scripture, thereby participating thoughtfully in groundwork reflection for a sermon sequence entitled "Encounters with the Person of Jesus."

Regardless of the form, the seminar has values for the participants, the preachers, and the parish. A letter from a professional writer, now living away from the area, witnesses to several facets of personal enrichment:

The seminars did indeed mean a great deal to me during a time of strain and it is difficult to put into words the combination of emotional and intellectual factors involved. . . .

At first I think I came with the idea of bettering my pitifully inadequate knowledge of the Bible. And perhaps at first I stayed just for the sake of a good argument, which I always enjoy. But it ultimately dawned on me that the Bible was far more closely related to life—and to my life—than I had ever realized before.

In time something else happened. The word "fellowship" is bandied about a church to a considerable extent, but it never had any very special meaning to me. It was a group of people. Ours is a large parish, and while I am not a shy person I always had the feeling of sitting around on the edges in a rather useless manner. The sermon seminars changed that. And I came to feel that I had been really knitted into the fabric of a fellowship—a close group of people who were all searching for clues to a closer relationship to God. It was a most supportive feeling, particularly at a time when my normal life pattern had been shattered rather badly.

Finally, and this took a long time to develop, prayer took on a new dimension. Whether it was a sense of the closeness of the group or because our minds had been stretched by the personal effort of discussion I don't know. But I know it was true for me. There were some nights when it had an intensity that was almost electric.

Other benefits have accrued. The preacher of the week is grateful for profound observations which bring depth of personal insight, and no less for trivia that enlarge the range of interest, thus providing bridges which enable him to reach people at points familiar to them. The contributions come from many sources. One sermon which students received with particular gratitude was made lively and relevant for them through subtle use of an incident recounted quite casually by a well-to-do, retired, conservative member of the group with whom the college crowd would normally have thought they had little in common. Preliminary discussion has served to increase receptivity and ease tensions when sermons have dealt with controversy. Lay insistence on the ambiguity of moral decisions kept one sermon in process from missing the mark. Again and again the seminar contributes vital touches of realism to the growing sermon. Sometimes as the group confronts the text, new themes emerge which must be dealt with in later sermons. Thus, in many and varied ways, the church's preaching is enriched and the scriptures are opened more widely to a waiting people.

The coin, however, has two sides. Persons who participate in the discussions are invariably eager to hear the sermon when Sunday comes around, for we know well the minister's continuing labor with the text may reveal a message quite different from anything we have discussed. Nor has the Word ceased to work in us. In what manner will it be spoken later? The preacher's indebtedness to the prior conversation is occasionally quite open; more often it is reflected only in a particular shading, a word or a touch of reality which coming from one person's life leads into another's. Clearly this is a far cry from a "sermon from a committee," as it was once erroneously described.

The seminar is often enlarged during Lent, when the number of participants once increased from thirty-five to between 150 and 200. Fifteen minutes of radio time scheduled on a local station enabled minister and organist to reach parishioners gathered in groups in neighborhood homes. Here the people followed the exegesis, joined as they wished in the singing of a hymn, united in prayers, then continued as seminars for forty-five minutes. This procedure led to a lively sense of the binding of the congregation. Leaders—some lay, some clergy—met in advance to prepare for the sessions, and each was responsible for forwarding insights to the minister, often by coming to his home at the close of the evening. During several lenten seasons a section has met in the church at 7:00 A.M. for a chapel service, a simple breakfast, and the seminar. Students, faculty members, and professional people enjoy these early gatherings; there the sense of fellowship runs high.

What is offered through this program is neither ordered Bible study nor prayer cell nor commitment group; yet it includes elements of each. We are convinced of the rightness of the principle and are gratified to hear reports of rich experiences with similar ventures in other churches, where patterns are wisely tailored to each situation. A constant element is the responsible involvement of the people of God with the Word of God. Through such encounter the Word becomes the enlightener and the enabler in the lives of men and women as they face their daily tasks and their mission in and to the world.

CHAPTER 7

BEYOND ACTIVISM

(This chapter first appeared as an article in *The Christian Century* in February 1968. Details of the outward scene have changed and may change again in quite unpredictable ways even before these pages are in print. The Haight-Ashbury district, for example, ceased to be a haven for hippies when the "smashers" took over the streets. As it comes to life again now it is assuming a different character marked by fresh signs of caring. All over the country communes multiply, taking many forms. Each one is a challenge to the church as an experiment in openness and as an expression of longing for relationship in an atmosphere of noncompetitive living. So the address of the culture to the church and the church to the culture remains. Names of avenues and districts, of drugs and cults may be altered to match time and circumstance, but the living church, wherever it may be, must keep eyes and ears and heart open to the cry from the city streets. Nevertheless, ministry to "the world" will be sterile unless it makes room for renewal through the sacraments of the religious spirit which brought it into being.)

Horrible and hopeful things are to be seen on the streets of our land: carnivals and riots, houses replaced by roaring freeways, alleys filled with overflowing garbage, new play-

"Beyond Activism" is reprinted by permission from the February 7, 1968 issue of *The Christian Century*. Copyright 1968 Christian Century Foundation.

grounds, restrictions on parking, unparalleled traffic jams, noise and smoke, songs and weeping—up out of the streets, urban incense to fill the nostrils of God. As the sweet and bitter fumes swirl among the seraphim, the church—the people of God—listens and worries and wonders and seeks to respond, to be "relevant," aware of Martin Buber's warning that "he who ceases to make a response ceases to hear the word."

So a good-sized chunk of American Protestant leadership has sought to be responsible—that is, to *respond*. In many quarters the church is being judged by the extent of its involvement in the world—which is quite as it should be. Yet, somehow the suspicion persists that something is lacking. Action-oriented congregations frequently dissolve into advocates of a vague humanism; again and again their leaders turn to Marx or LSD, or to instruments for social change they consider more effective than the church. Is something more than activism demanded? Is activism by itself a dead-end street, as some have begun to suspect? Is there nothing beyond increased secular involvement for substantial mainline Protestantism with its study groups, dialogue sermons, social action seminars, imaginative mission boards, and a conscience about civil rights and Vietnam and ecumenicity?

Two street scenes in contemporary American life present an unspoken but crucial challenge to every Christian activist, every culturally earnest church in the land. They deserve to be observed closely.

CHALLENGED BY THE DISHEVELED

One of those scenes is to be observed at the corner of two streets—Haight and Ashbury in San Francisco and at every Haight-Ashbury confluence in every city of the land. In this scene are young people in beards and long hair and sandals, rebelling against the Establishment, against the government and civil service, and the church and university. It is a scene by no means confined to San Francisco or Berkeley or the East Village; it is one breaking out in little pockets across the land. In this scene are troubled youngsters, from teeny-boppers to youth well past college age, playing out their childhood in costume, covering their rage and inadequacy with a shocking, public no-saying and thus managing a yes-saying—a yes-saying which establishes at last a brash but trembling personhood.

The word this strange subculture delivers to the church is a word about religion—its necessity, its ritual, its distortion, its high priests. To sophisticated theologians who talk about a "religionless Christianity" this scene sends its spokesman with a word about a "Christianityless religion." Its actors do not see it as such; they often accord high honor to Jesus, the gentle teacher, while scorning religion in any organized sense. But Christianity knows more than a gentle teacher; it *is* organized, it *is* people bound together.

SERVICE AND ADORATION

These disheveled rebels bring a strong question and a strong rebuke; they make the church uneasy, for many are gentle and many are generous. As to LSD, that dangerous instrument of an instant and automated religion, they may well refer to the prophet Joel as he is quoted in Acts 2:17: "Your young men shall see visions, and your old men shall dream dreams." But then, to the discomfort and dismay of Bible-reading Christians, they *live* out the rest of that apostolic chapter, holding "all things in common," selling their goods and distributing "them to all, as any [has] need (Acts 2:44–45)." In San Francisco the Diggers feed anyone who comes just for the sheer joy of sharing.

This new, twentieth-century American Gnosticism is a dreadful caricature of Christian faith. But like other caricatures, especially sincere and honest ones, it speaks a word of judgment to the churches: that a religion without ecstasy, without rapture is, as the saying goes, strictly for the birds.

My desk dictionary offers as the first definition of religion: "The service and adoration of God or a god expressed in forms of worship." The early Christians were possessed by love; they disregarded property because they had undergone a transforming, ecstatic experience of personal encounter with the living God. Their lives were drawn together and were characterized by an extraordinary dimension: the vertical line marking divine visitation, a line overflowing with human response in adoration of God. Their religion was not religion without this at its heart; it was there not only as an individual experience but as the distinguishing mark, the unabated source of cohesion and power for their *corporate* life.

The new Gnostics of the hippy world demonstrate man's need for this dimension in existence, and their eagerness to accept disappointing and dangerous substitutes for it is a direct and painful word to the church. "But how else?" they ask us. "We have not found ecstasy among you!" If the church they judge and find wanting in this respect is the church of the sort I know, they are right!

NO ROOM FOR RAPTURE?
Wrote Langdon Gilkey:

The current movements of American theology are almost all in a secular direction. The more radical wing accepts this *in toto*, proclaiming the "death of God" in our time and the consequent need for Christian faith and for theology to proceed—without reference to God— in building itself entirely around the figure of Jesus and his call to service in the world.[1]

Then Gilkey sounded a significant warning: American religion "faces the problem of retaining a *religious* dimension in its now secularized church life and theology; it is by no means certain that such a churchly tradition can continue to be fruitful if it loses all touch with its trans-cultural sources."[2]

In its effort to be in touch with transcultural sources, the sick but sincere mechanical ecstasy of the hippy subculture underlines the emptiness and embarrassment of contemporary mainline Protestantism about worship, prayer, preaching, and the sacraments. It is commonly assumed that we have turned from those traditional "means of grace" because they have proved ineffectual and inoperative, that pulpit dialogue and group therapy and public demonstrations have appeared to us more promising. But could the truth be that these latter-day agents have simply seemed less threatening? One can bury himself deeply in them without the danger of having one's heart "strangely warmed."

It is well to remember that the means of grace, even the traditional ones, enable the living Christ to warm our hearts. And when that happens, the heart-warming is not just a *private* affair. For this is not ecstasy like that of the hippies, accompanied by ethical nearsightedness; it is rapture not shorn of moral imperative but rather born of it and interlaced with it—as joy may rest hidden in grief, may shine brightest in sorrow's tears. Was it not for the "joy that was set before him" that Jesus endured the cross, despising the shame?

The foundations of the thresholds shake at that voice, and like Isaiah we cry out "Woe is me" and try to look the other way. In recent years some Christian secularists have sought to persuade us that our religious ceremonies themselves, all the paraphernalia of worship—candles and choirs and crosses, ushers and preachers and hymns—can simply serve to hide us from that experience. Often, indeed, that is so. No one who has refereed theological students on the liturgical diamond with the General Confession scored in basic English would argue that point! But *that* bypass of Divine Encounter may be far less treacherous than the ambush into which we are being led by that sort of Christian secularism which insists that there is no better place to meet Christ than out in the world, in the secular city where the action is. Who is going to introduce us? The truth may be that there is no better place to *hide* from Christ than in the midst of the city, if in the center of the city there is no bread broken in Christ's name, no scripture opened for him, and no hearts warmed by him.

First Congregational Church in Berkeley established and operated a Halfway House for young parolees in cooperation with the California Youth Authority. We saw it as part of our engagement with the world which we believed could not be delegated, not even to a well-managed and highly motivated denominational commission or interfaith council. In spite of manifold problems and constant crises, the doors of the house were closed only when state funds for the Youth Authority were critically curtailed. It now appears that experience gained by the church and the government agency in this enterprise will be increasingly valuable as local communities are once again assigned responsibility for transitional care and support of persons newly released from penal and mental institutions.

WHENCE COMES OUR INSPIRATION?

We were gratified that our college young people were attracted to this kind of service in the secular city, but our suspicions led us to raise with them the question of motivation. As a result, we came to require that everyone working in the project participate in what was dubbed an "action-reflection group." The participation uncovered much that good works had covered. We began to discover not only that such involvement does not necessarily proceed from, much less lead to, valid Christian experience, but—worse—that it can be a particularly subtle and secure hiding place from such experience.

The failure of churches like ours may lie not so much in their faltering attempts at social relevance as in their intellectually respectable but emotionally sterile life of worship and Christian nurture. Their failure to offer sensitive and idealistic young people the opportunity for emotionally stimulating and satisfying religious experience may well be one reason those young people turn from the church. We have assumed that they turned away because we were not socially relevant, were not sensitive to the great issues—race, war, injustice, poverty. So some parishes and some denominations and some theological schools have engaged in a deadly game —"How to be relevant without half praying."

I hate to think where we would be without at least this much of an earnest response to the claims of Christ on the church. But for the world's sake we need to ask where this new, young, beautiful generation is which we assumed would note our response and flock into our churches and reinvigorate our invasion of the secular city. One place the young people are not is in our dull, pedantic, emotionless services where one well-placed, well-modulated, well-articulated amen would shake the abortion pamphlets off the social action table and send the League of Women Voters running for cover. Don't misunderstand: I favor the legalizing of abortion and I greatly admire the League of Women Voters; but such concerns are the *consequence* of Christian faith, not its *substance*. Paul Tillich's warning may well be heeded: The church must avoid that secular desecration of Protestantism which occurs "when it replaces ecstasy with doctrinal or moral structure."

The next time you meet members of the long-hair-and-sandal sect in New York or Berkeley or on your television screen, you may be strangely startled to recall the last place you saw people dressed like that—at the Sunday school

Christmas pageant! The cry for the church to "get into the world" is mocked by this strange Christmas-pageant procession on the streets of our cities. That scene warns us that a religion without ecstasy, without rapture, without a strange warming of the heart is indeed one for the birds.

CHURCHMEN WHO RESPOND

Even as we try to absorb that warning, our attention is drawn to another contemporary street scene: the sight of ordained Christians, the set-apart ministry, out in many exposed places, in the horrible and hopeful things that have been happening on the streets of the world. Many of these men and women have been brought face to face with the renewing power of Christ re-presented to them and sparked to life within them by the discipline of the church's witness in its "churchly tradition." They have been subjected to what Robert McAfee Brown calls the spirit of Protestantism: "An openness to the judging and renewing activity of the Living God made known in Jesus Christ." In the past twenty-five years they have developed a courageous, relevant, tough, cutting-edge ministry in many a campus center and coffeehouse, in many an urban and rural slum.

The men and women of whom I write have been supported and inspired by the informed, sensitive, and creative leadership of the national boards of some denominations and by councils of churches—in a fashion often not possible by local churches. They have marched and suffered; some have died. Some have become celebrated martyrs; more have remained careful, quiet, hard-hitting saints of the church. They have armed themselves with the tools of enlightened urban sociology, the wisdom of practical politics, the skills of the psychologist and teacher and social worker.

Like John Howard, the great British penal reformer who was trusted by the imprisoned whom he wished to help because he moved in among them and became as they were—

imprisoned—these men and women have become part of the streets from Harlem to Watts, have developed new ministries, have given new meaning and glory to the word incarnation. They have offered the single, most persuasive evidence in our time of the spirit of Protestantism, evidence of the "renewing activity of the Living God made known in Jesus Christ." No wonder the current generation of student seminarians, for the most part, honors the prophet and despises the priest!

THE "SOMETHING MORE"

But there is hidden in this scene, as in the scene peopled by the hippies, a grave warning, a danger signal which activist, secular, religionless Christianity might be inclined to overlook were it not for the conspicuous Haight-Ashbury scene. For if we trace the personal religious history of these avant-garde clergy of the streets, we find that almost to a man they were once somehow personally subjected to the "judging and renewing activity of the Living God made known in Jesus Christ." The "churchly tradition" was transmitted to them; and in its midst they were confronted by the claims of God gathered up in the cross and played out anew for every generation in the reading of scripture, in the singing of hymns, in the recitation of divine acts, in the bread and wine, and in their constant reenactment in the preaching of the Word. There was Christ-oriented and disciplined ecstasy in their experience. Somewhere, somehow the channels were, by the grace of God, sufficiently unclogged for these modern saints and martyrs to hear the Word and to be empowered to obey its demands. There is something *beneath* activism which suggests there must also be something beyond it.

The question which the development of the clergy of the streets addresses to the church is this: Are the new, "relevant," secular ministries providing for the continuance of that Protestant spirit of which they themselves are the creation?

Is there incorporated into their life style, their discipline, their worship the means for constant renewal of the church at the hands of God, to the end that activism itself may be reformed and renewed? It seems to me imperative that the people engaged in such ministries must either gather together the community God calls to break the bread, be subject to the discipline of the scripture and thus be the church with its renewing secret, or so engage their ministry that it openly and regularly repairs to such a community.

For the Protestant principle of renewal is specific and real, as Christ is specific and bread is real. When such ministries provide for the reenactment of Christ's presence (and why else are some Christians set apart by ordination?), even though that reenactment may take place in the most un-Gothic surroundings and may make use of the most unorthodox elements, the church is there with its renewing secret. But it must be gathered in Christ's name, and without the scripture and the tradition it cannot know that name. Ultimately that is the manner of his identification; none other has been provided. The Christian faith is a historical faith; it is not absorbed philosophically out of the atmosphere or lifted existentially out of a mystic trance.

Ministry to the world which is not anchored in the sacramental life of the community of faith tends, perhaps inadvertently, to provide what Michael Harrington has called the "if you can't lick 'em, join 'em" approach.

The Church . . . must, to be sure, fight for the earthly implication of the heavenly values it affirms; it can never again divorce God from the Negroes, the poor, those dying in war and the rest of humanity. But over and above that witness to the temporal meetings of the eternal there must be the assertion of the eternal itself. And, amid all the showmanship and swinging theology, this is what I miss.[3]

If the church does not show forth the dimensions of the eternal in its common life, how will it—let alone the world—

know its Lord or feel the demands and comfort of perfect love?

THE CONSEQUENCE OF CHRIST'S PRESENCE

In the introduction to the World Council of Churches' recently published report on the missionary structure of the congregation, titled *The Church for Others,* the editor recalls the passage in a German novel which describes a man watching a woman on the street. Something in her appearance strikes him; he follows her into a flower shop and to the streetcar station. Then: "All of a sudden he realizes that he has followed his own wife, with whom he had spent the whole night. But he had not recognized her." [4] In this report, the editor continues, the North American working group of the World Council study is asking the question: "How can we recognize —in the flower shop, at the street-car stop, in the slums of the big cities, in the cinema, in the picket line—that same Christ, whose body we have shared at the Lord's table?" [5]

Well, the answer to that question would seem to me to begin with the suggestion that it would be quite a feat for one to recognize his wife in the crowd if he had not first wooed her and claimed her and known her as wife. Yet, again and again, we seem to be following the secular logic which would hold that the discipline of the knowledge of Christ in scripture and tradition, in word and sacrament, in fellowship and experience must be forsaken so we can have time and energy to pursue him in the flower shop and the cinema and the slum. That pursuit—the church on the move—must not be neglected, but it must be undertaken as a *consequence* of Christ's dwelling within us, not in order to conceal his absence.

THE CONGREGATIONAL IMPERATIVE

The World Council report concludes with an account of three projects of the church in the San Francisco area. It details the common motivation and purpose of the three different plans—one providing for a "dialogue between religion and the arts," one seeking to meet the need of young adults for "belonging," one designed to engage Christian scientists and engineers in responsible social action. It explains that "from a structural viewpoint there was no choice for each of the projects but to develop at a distance from local congregations in order to be or to become truly open for the purpose and the people whom they were to serve." [6] In the next paragraph we read that "somehow, the distance from the church as a structure also seemed to entail a distance from, and almost a break with, Christian tradition." [7] And finally: "Thus the present anti-theological bias present in these projects might be regarded as a first step toward a more truly theological stance, conducive to their open-ended purpose." [8]

Indeed, so it might be; we must discover some means to overcome the handicaps which the image of the culturally stained contemporary congregation imposes on Christ's mission. In these three projects, deliberately divorced from that tradition, we may very well discern a warning about the dead-end street which Christian mission may enter when the missioners pursue an antitheological bias and turn their backs on local structures. Six months after the date affixed to that introduction an earnest inquiry about the three projects was made among liberal clergymen in San Francisco. It is sobering and instructive to note that of those three plans one was lying fallow and the others were finding continued usefulness difficult apart from the structured church.

The resigned director of one of these projects was quoted in a local newspaper to the effect that "even the churches' social action programs are 'more in terms of doing things for people than in providing spiritual guidance.'" His comment came in the course of a report on a one-day symposium on "The Religious Significance of Psychedelic Drugs" organized by the University of California medical center. The reporter

94

observed that "while the spiritual claims of the psychedelics were described in generous terms, there pervaded at the symposium a yearning for the organized church to take hold of its lost flocks."

Well, I should say so! It is for that very compelling reason that as the people of God listen seriously to the warning from the streets, they must hear with the ears of those who believe that God has not left his people in any age or in this one without signs and symbols, without direction, without means of renewal at his gracious hand.

CHAPTER 8

EDUCATION FOR MINISTRY IN THE LOCAL CHURCH

Some of my best friends are seminary professors or seminary students or administrators! Among them and their colleagues are heroic souls who are trying, against tremendous odds, to develop schools where men and women can be adequately prepared for leadership in the local church in America today. But alas, their efforts are mostly too little and too late. Drastic, radical reform of education for the parish ministry is long overdue.

This does not mean that many notable and internationally known centers of theological education are not doing an important work. They are. They are expanding the sum total of knowledge of religion and society; they are exploring Christianity and the arts. They are training scholars, teachers, journalists, social scientists, psychological counselors, and theological educators. Indeed, some of these schools have become centers for political action and for immediate and direct reform of business, industry, politics, and higher education. One enrollee in an eastern seminary is reported to have expressed surprise when someone mentioned "classes." He

"Education for Ministry in the Local Church" is reprinted by permission from the January 27, 1971 issue of *The Christian Century* ("Lineaments of Seminary Renewal"). Copyright 1971 Christian Century Foundation.

thought the school was simply a crash pad for youthful revolutionaries in that metropolitan area. But this is parenthetical. The point is that all this work is being done in schools originally established for training ministers for local congregations.

WHAT ABOUT THE CHURCH ON THE CORNER?

This former role of seminaries—especially in the more prestigious schools outside the South—has now become so peripheral a part of their total educational scene as to be almost lost in the enthusiastic shuffle toward "relevant" ministries in campus center and vineyard scene, in coffeehouse and council chamber. It seems increasingly unlikely that very many of these schools now possess the motivation or the capacity for the sort of radical reorganization which would be required to make them useful again in preparing men and women as ministers of the local, gathered congregation in both its traditional and evolving forms.

Their resistance to such reform is not a matter of unwillingness to change. (Who can name a school not currently rearranging its academic or administrative furniture?) Rather, their resistance arises from their commitment and fealty to the academic establishment and its intellectual presuppositions and vested interests. (Note the frantic concern of the American Association of Theological Schools in regard to the degree member schools should confer.) That academic orientation, as against "church" or even "gospel" orientation, has deepened in recent years, at equal pace with the growth of doubt about the viability of the congregation and the lowering of the cultural status of the ministry. To expect these schools all at once to put their main energies and funds into training ministers for local congregations is totally unrealistic. Not only is the work they are now performing essential for the church and the gospel; many such schools are strongly influenced at all levels by leaders, official and unofficial, who quite honestly believe that it is a waste of time to try to raise up a ministry for the church on the corner.

However, evidence is now increasing that the church on the corner may be pivotal in the wider ecclesiastical scene. Treasurers of the denominations, the mission boards, and the councils of churches are at one in suggesting that there will be scant opportunity for all special ministries—from the most traditional missionary assignment to the most "far out" street ministry—if we do not dramatically enhance the effectiveness and enlarge the Christian vision of the local church. As of now, that is a fundamental and vexing problem for the church in America, and there are many places where it must be tackled. Certainly *one* place to get a fingerhold on this problem is at the point of professional leadership of the local congregation. And one place to tackle *that* probem is in the schools which largely influence the training of that leadership.

About two years ago a third-year student at a leading divinity school, William J. Horvath, announced in the pages of *The Christian Century* (June 24, 1970) that some of his classmates were going into parishes as ministers just to "give it a try." He and his friends had come to this horrendous professional decision as a matter of necessity, inasmuch as the budgets for specialized ministries have been severely cut. One commiserates with the bewildered congregations blessed with foot-dragging aspirants to leadership who "intend to be outspoken in their pronouncements" and will not tolerate a senior pastor or "a laity longing for the past." Yet, we must not expend all our sympathy on such congregations. A good share of it will have to go to these aspirants, because men and women who enter into the life and leadership of a congregation so tentatively and critically are heading for a hard time, and few will survive it. Such a relationship holds about as much promise as a marriage in which the ceremony includes negotiations about who shall have custody of the wedding cake.

MEDIOCRITY NOT THE ONLY MODEL

Yet one can hardly blame these able and concerned young people for their lack of enthusiasm. All across this land there is local church after local church which appears to emit only the slightest flicker of light in dreadfully dark places. Also, the quality of men in the parish ministry is nothing to brag about. Although such evaluations are highly subjective, no one would contend that the most promising of our youths in the past twenty years have been drawn to the ministry. There is large comfort in believing that the Almighty can make do with very ordinary material. But while such "spiritualizing" of the low caliber of the ministry may console those of us who are ministers, it doesn't do much for drawing able candidates! Those graduating seminarians are not really as arrogant as they sound when they write so condescendingly about the average congregation and its minister. These are not a very happy sight!

However, is such mediocrity their only possible model? I think of a well-prepared and hard-working minister in a mid-American town of under 2,500 persons. He has been there nine years, declining several opportunities to "improve himself." He continues a daily discipline of study and prayer, and Sunday he preaches very substantially to a congregation of blue-collar and white-collar people who, in the course of those nine years, have discovered how much power they possess to neutralize the mid-American mind in their town (a town that posted at its boundaries a "Keep U.S. out of U.N." sign and once gave a free haircut to a "student" passing through).

That congregation is a creative counterforce in that town —in the schools, in the local council, in the columns of the weekly newspaper. And that minister has helped it to develop this potential, not through outspoken pronouncements, but through the faithful development of relations with and enlightened pastoral care of his people, and through his effective teaching of the Bible and his ability to translate the faith of our fathers into the language of our children. That is to say, he has won the trust and affection of his people. Had he come in declaring that he had no patience with laymen seeking comfort and resolved to make pronouncements out of his vast specialized knowledge, he would never have seen what minister and people *together* can do and be: a Christian presence in the heart of the nation. By this time he would probably be off where the action is, where God is speaking "on street corners and in the ghettos, in storefronts, factories, community organizations and coffeehouses"—having earned the martyr's badge pinned on him by his peers. But he stayed with a far less pretentious ministry, and he has seen himself multiplied as an agent, a minister, of God's gospel. He has been multiplied *through* a congregation of people spread *through* a whole community and reaching, *through* one of its members, into the state legislature, where with their encouragement he is now fighting some dangerous, new, redneck legislation.

To cite such a case is not to deny the validity of specialized ministries. In the past decade such ministries have won an effective press and the interest of despairing youth as very few general ministries have. They have produced many genuine and self-effacing heroes. True, it may be useful sometimes not to be self-effacing; and it certainly requires a sort of brash heroism to scream "pig" at an "overreacting" policeman in a liberal university community. But apparently there are many candidates for that kind of heroism among the young today. Another sort of heroism is needed in the lonely outpost, in the midst of ordinary "law-abiding" citizens where many young people who enter the parish ministry

101

find themselves. But that heroism consists not in seeing how soon they can get run out of town but in seeing how soon that local community of believers can make a "Christian" difference in the lives of its members and, *through* them, in the world around them.

TO HEAL A SICK SOCIAL ORDER

All at once we seem to have rediscovered that vast sweep of ordinary citizens, the great American middle and lower-middle class, with its fears and apprehensions—a body politic against whose inclination no resolve or legislation for reform can prevail. If it be argued that seminaries supply clergymen primarily for liberal upper classes, not for angry lower classes, then it would be well to take seriously Michael Novak's essay "Healing Class Tensions in a Sick Society." Writing in the aftermath of the Kent State tragedy, Novak notes the rage of the hard-hats and of all those citizens who are "sick and tired of all this protest crap," and wonders whether "the cry 'All power to the people!' (will not) one day haunt the radical movement. For *the difficulty with our new populists is that between them and the people there are very few good vibrations.*" [1] Cynthia Wedel, president of the National Council of Churches, underlines a similar fact of life. She writes: "As modern theology swept through the seminaries and produced a new breed of clergymen dedicated to demonstrating the gospel's relevance to a changing world, no one thought of the millions of church people who still lived in another theological world." [2]

Novak puts forth concrete suggestions toward the creative healing of our sick social order. Some healing that is needed, he suggests, can come only through the efforts of the middle-aged and aging upper-middle classes in which our average, mainline Protestant churches seem to specialize. He sees a crucial task to be done by the sort of people who *comfortably*

102

fill our traditional churches and Sunday after Sunday lament the absence of the youth. Ralph Sockman once defined a "comfortably filled" church as one with enough room in the pews for everyone to lie down and be comfortable. Be that as it may, the truth remains that the healing of our society involves a task for which even a largely youthless congregation is well fitted. But where is the professional leadership to nurture such congregations? Responsibility for the absence of strong leadership cannot be laid exclusively at the door of the seminary. The whole church is to blame and the whole church must be concerned with effective remedies. After all, seminaries work only with the people the churches supply. But where can we get a handhold on the problem? Where can the unfortunate cycle of ineffectualness be most readily broken?

It seems increasingly plain to me that theological schools might be the quickest and most effective place to begin, if for no other reason than that a school affords a controlled and concentrated situation. The churches themselves are far too diffuse and separated. Further, the problem is essentially related to leadership, and presumably it would be possible for some theological school to forego the prestige and luxury of a multifaceted curriculum and decide to concentrate all its resources on training of men and women of all ages, races, and religious persuasions for the ministry of local congregations.

Of course, there are many schools which are primarily concerned with the training of ministers. But the drift in schools that are most conspicuous on the theological scene (again, outside the South) has been to do everything but train men for the realities of local congregations. And why not? If Mr. Horvath has his figures straight, 80 percent of his class said they did not plan to work in a parish. They said this when they *arrived* at seminary. A school accepting such students could scarcely fulfill its responsibility to them if it only offered training for a profession 80 percent did not intend to follow. So these splendid theological schools have moved farther and farther away from substantial intentional training for the local church. We all may rejoice that they have become such outstanding centers for purely intellectual disciplines, on the one hand, and for specialized training of counselors and educators and professional scholars on the other. It would be difficult and perhaps wasteful for them to reorganize themselves in the radical fashion required if they are to get at the problem of a poorly trained ministry in a faltering church. It may be best to recognize them for what they are, leave them in the arms of the universities whose embrace they so eagerly seek, and establish more modest operations for persons who wish to commit themselves to the discipline and opportunity of parish ministry. I am sure most local churches would not be troubled by the absence of proper academic credentials if the minister possessed demonstrable professional competence.

A CLEAR VOCATIONAL ASSUMPTION

It is not enough, however, to say that radical reform in the training of parish clergy is urgent. People in positions of responsibility in theological education have a right to ask the parochial critic what such a renewed training center might look like, what its distinguishing characteristics would be. Let me cite three characteristics which I believe would be extremely important for such a new or reformed school to possess.

First, its life would be marked by a thorough but not uncritical commitment to the church in its specific and local manifestation. For example, it would be clearly understood that if you enrolled in this school you would be treated as though you were preparing to be a parish minister. You would not be encouraged to come simply to explore the Christian faith (though such continued exploration would be inevitable); you would not be encouraged to come if your vocational intent were clearly "to teach Bible at the college level" (though skills for teaching Bible would be seriously developed). Thus the school would be guided by a clear, vocational assumption.

It has long troubled me that a primary requirement for receiving one of the few substantial fellowships established to bring abler persons into the ministry is vocational indecision. The high intent and hopeful focus of that requirement are to be applauded. Nonetheless, it makes indecisiveness (a deadly trait in the ministry) one absolute for eligibility. Then it arranges for its winning applicants to spend a year in a seminary to decide if the parish ministry is their cup of tea! Miracle enough if the vocational resolve of men already committed to the parish survives a year in many seminaries!

How exciting a school would be if it had the focus of vocational commitment—commitment not to a traditional ministry but to the reality and promise of the gathered congregation as the "real church." Every student would understand this basic premise whether he was ready to accept it personally or not. And if undecided persons found it unpalatable, they could go to other seminaries or graduate schools of religion until they really wanted to prepare for parish leadership.

The school's faculty and administrators would also need to be committed to the parish church. They would need to agree with Hans Küng that the local church "is in no way to be seen as a subdivision of the real 'Church.' The whole Church can only be understood in terms of the local Church and its concrete actions. The local Church . . . is the real Church." [3] Understandably, this requirement of commitment might lead one to think that such a school would insist on something tantamount to a loyalty oath and would inevitably become ingrown. Such dangers are real. But the effort to steer away from them is partly responsible for the present plight of seminaries—one in which many influential professors and students know next to nothing about an ordinary parish church or any gathered community of Christian faith. They do not even join with the seminary community for prayer. This kind of situation may be healthy in a graduate school of religion, but in a professional school a handful of such persons surely would be sufficient. They may even be useful in the way a Christian Science practitioner can be useful in a medical school to help keep orthodox medicine "on its toes," so to speak. But most medical schools would be extremely reluctant to have Christian Scientists manning most key positions.

A FUNCTIONAL CURRICULUM

The second characteristic of a renewed theological school is that it will have a functional curriculum—one whose courses are oriented toward professional preparation of ministers. Such a curriculum will deliver the school from the legitimate sort of criticism recently leveled against police training programs. Robert Rubin, producer of films designed to help policemen become realistic about themselves and their work, has said: "Police recruits are getting a bad shake because most police training courses are dishonest—they simply don't tell them what they're going to find in the streets." [4] A functional curriculum would not simply tack on a few "practical courses"; every discipline would be explored in terms of vocational realities, in terms of what ministers-to-be will soon find "in the streets" and pews.

For example, some of the best preaching courses I ever participated in were taught by professors of the Old and New Testaments. Higher criticism and *Heilsgeschichte* were taught in those courses, but both Bible and preaching were approached with the understanding that the students were preparing to be parish ministers, not regent professors of biblical archaeology! If such an approach were to be pursued seriously today, it would doubtless entail retooling on the part of the scholars in the specific disciplines. Such retooling might very well include the requirement that alternate sabbatical leaves be spent deep in the heart, not of Switzerland or Palestine but of a local congregation.

A functional curriculum will require instructors who know a great deal about human motivation; under such a curriculum, seminars in the ministry's essential disciplines would be conducted so as to foster not only mastery of the subject matter but also skill in working with people. The inseparability of content and method would be explicitly acknowledged; hence, extensive joint teaching is likely to be called for, and certainly there would have to be tremendous mutuality and confidence among the faculty. A school with a functional curriculum could hardly hope to succeed unless the faculty's commitment to its common task and to one another is more determinative of personal priorities than are the temptations of individual distinction as a scholar or financial achievement as a popular lecturer or writer.

THE NECESSITY OF SUBJECTIVITY

Finally, a reformed theological school would depend as much on "the rhythmic, earthy, and emotive" as on the intellectual and analytical, as much on the reality of "subjective" as of "objective" experience. The Ph.D. model would be retired to the university museum—and along with it the tedious debate about what letters should be used to designate the degree to be conferred.

We are children of an age that has come to a dead end. Initiated in the seventeenth century, the age is now experiencing a spiritual showdown in the form of a schism between the world of religion and the world of science, between the world of poetry and the world of chemistry. It is an age in which we have had drummed into us from earliest childhood—at home, at school, at play—that the only adequate and trustworthy categories of experience are the rational, the objective, the demonstrable, the provable. The ineffectiveness of a church nurtured by leaders trained under these presuppositions is evident in the deadlines of the majority of America's liberal, educated congregations.

We churchmen have assumed, for instance, that in order to know Jesus one first must examine all the objective data available—the records, the stories, the traditions, the archaeological finds—and then eliminate everything that does not seem to be beyond reasonable doubt. By means of this process we have concluded that the only reliable knowledge about Jesus—and thus the only real Jesus—is somehow "out there." He is not real and present as "Jesu, Joy of Man's Desiring"; he is not real as he has been infinitely expanded in the hearts and lives of his followers—in the apostles and martyrs, in Augustine and Wesley and Pope John XXIII. No, he is real only in the objective, verifiable fact of his short existence in the flesh. That process has reduced Jesus to a few short lines and has reduced preaching to teaching and holy communion to a moment of memory. The so-called "objectiveness" that is the curse of our age has closed down at least half our receiving apparatus to the gift of the Spirit. And is not that the gift for the lack of which we are wasting away?

In a superb recent lecture, Hazaiah Williams, director of urban-black studies at Graduate Theological Union in Berkeley, spelled out the instinctive wisdom of the black church in this regard. The black church, he said, comes out of an African culture which views reality quite differently than does the European; "rhythmic, earthy, emotive," the black church lives out in its worship the understanding that emotionality is

108

as legitimate as rationality in the authentication of reality. And Williams went on to protest the high-flown rational pursuits which say nothing to the spirit.

Whereas once I prayed for the thorough integration of the black church and the white—as a matter of racial justice and as a witness to the secular community—I now suspect that the Almighty may have preserved the black church, "rhythmic, earthy, emotive," at the living heart of twentieth-century Protestantism in order to save the whole church with its presumptuous and dead-ending objectivity.

A community of learning which does not acknowledge and search out and rely upon this sort of "subjective" knowledge —"rhythmic, earthy, emotive"—cannot possibly be adequate to prepare men and women for the ministry of the church of Christ in this or any age, regardless of what form that ministry takes.

Where is the wise man? Where is the scribe? Where is the debater of this age? Has not God made foolish the wisdom of the world? For since, in the wisdom of God, the world did not know God through wisdom, it pleased God through the folly of what we preach to save those who believe. For Jews demand signs and Greeks seek wisdom, but we preach Christ crucified, a stumbling-block to Jews and folly to Gentiles, but to those who are called, both Jews and Greeks, Christ the power of God and the wisdom of God.

—1 Corinthians 1:20–24

CHAPTER 9

TO EQUIP GOD'S
PEOPLE FOR WORK
IN HIS SERVICE

"Where two or three have met together in my name," said Jesus, "I am there among them." Moved by hope or habit or by some haunting remembrance of this promise the people come. They come from their farms and retirement retreats to the meeting house at a country crossroad or assemble in some bravely steepled edifice at an urban intersection, or kneel in a proud cathedral at a city's center. Buildings there are as places of meeting, but Christ's presence can no more be confined in a building than he himself could be confined to ministering in the courtyard of the temple. The foregoing chapters press the claim that these people are the church and precisely for that reason they must be abroad in the world to be a Christian presence there. But how shall they be Christ's presence unless they are equipped? And how shall they be equipped unless they be captured by Christ, enraptured by him and engaged with him?

The local church was defined as "any group of persons who come together in the name of Jesus Christ, seeking to be open to his presence and obedient to his spirit" (chapter 3). The words may draw assent readily enough, but in fact it is no casual matter to come together in the name of Jesus Christ; nor is it easy for anyone to open himself to another, let alone to one whom even strong men have recognized as Lord. And as for obedience, the word itself is suspect in an age when authority has been toppled from its pedestal. There is need to question more closely, then, the gathering, the self-opening, and the response.

THE GATHERING

A culture which cares more for contemporaneity than for constancy bestows names as it bestows honors—for a season. Witness how school names change with the waxing and waning of stars of public education. Even the names of major cities change with changing politics: St. Petersburg—Petrograd—Leningrad. But the church bears its name in the biblical sense in which *name* is indistinguishable from *person*. To come together in Christ's name is to come together in his presence; and if we are in his presence, what happens there must perforce be an experience with him.

An experience with Christ? We want our experience of Christ to be separate and unearthly. We dream of being translated into some unique state, no longer subject to human irritation or defilement. Can we expect to meet Jesus Christ among dull people at dreary services in drab churches? or among the socially elite before some candle-lit altar on Cathedral Heights? Indeed, where else do we expect to meet him? That is precisely where he is always found, among quite ordinary people, among hungering, longing, limping people wherever and whenever they meet together and call on his name. Jesus surrounded himself with no company of either spiritual specialists or compatible companions. Even the little record we have of the chosen twelve shows the familiar range of human foibles. These men, as different from one another as they could be, were quarrelsome, jealous, irritable, irritating, sometimes doubting, sometimes dull, quick of temper, and slow of heart. Yes, but they were more than this. Jesus saw them as God's people and called them together to equip them for work in his service. They had a tendency to want to take this as being called to special honor. Will I sit at your right hand in the kingdom? It was, in fact, the disciples who were closest to Jesus who thought they could enshrine him in a booth on a mountaintop. But he promptly led them back to the valley, to the humdrum people there to join those other disciples who had been so eager to do good works on their own in his absence that they had even neglected to pray, forgetting in their confidence that the power to redeem life is divine. Present-day disciples are no different, as is soon discovered, even in Christian bodies gathered explicitly as companies of the committed.

The people who first came to Jesus were drawn for assorted reasons. Some came because they were sick or sick at heart or anxious or adrift; some because they knew their sin and could no longer bear the blinding burden of their guilt; some because they had ability or strength or intellect or wealth and wondered how to use it; some because the joy and meaning of their lives had died; some out of curiosity or intellectual eagerness. Some came because they caught a glimpse of glory.

It is still so, and we make strange company when we come together in our churches, incongruous company when seen objectively and incompatible surely, except as Christ is there.

THE SELF–OPENING

It is well and good to say that Christ is present in word and sacrament, but there is assuredly no set way in which the diverse company of seekers meet him and experience either his healing grace or his call to service. Too often they go away empty and unstirred. If the minister preaches the gospel and observes the sacraments in some historic form untouched by time, chances are his people will fail to hear the Word because the words and thought forms are a foreign tongue. The people will go through motions but will not receive the bread and wine as sacrament because they only observe the action as archaic ritual. If, on the other hand, the preacher speaks carelessly, offering his own convictions or his personal concern to comfort or berate or rouse his people, the people may be seen to flee or follow; but if the latter, it is more likely they will be following the leader than the Lord. And small wonder that the sacraments cease to be signs and agents of grace if we confuse the private and personal dedication of *our* child to God with public and grateful acknowledgment of God's prevenient love for *his* child; or if we mistake the pleasant refreshment of coffee and conversation after church for the joyous renewal promised to those who meet with the Lord at his table!

If the church is any group of persons who come together in the name of Jesus Christ, seeking to be open to his presence, those people must keep this intention paramount. Their rituals will be ordered as means of reenacting that presence in the present, recognizing that reenactment is not endless repetition of the past but living drama deeply rooted in both present and historical reality. So with worship—they will employ not one mode but many. Liberal Protestants have tended to overlook this need when we closed the doors on Wednesday-night prayer meetings and Sunday-evening vespers because they no longer served any purpose other than to perpetuate a pattern. But Sunday morning at eleven or ten or nine grows sterile also if it does not continue to speak both to and for the people and the Lord.

The good news comes from God. The forms must come from the people. Old-time Christians are no more apt to meet Christ through a rock band than the uninitiated are to encounter him by reading the Apostles' Creed; and yet ecstatic, lively, person-moving music is as valid and vital an expression of faith as are the formulae which set forth other men's experiences of God. One way to worship, then, is to divide ourselves by age and preference, but that is to impoverish everyone and to deny the universality of Christ. Ultimately we meet him only as he meets us together. Christianity is social, not private. Andrew, a tradesman, knew Jesus also through the experience of Matthew, who worked for the government; Peter had to face the discomfort of discovering that Jesus dealt differently with him than with John, yet called them both to common discipleship with him.

The gathered people who are speaking through this little volume make their discoveries just as other churches do. We discovered that double services for our central act of public worship, however appropriate they might seem as adjustment to capacity, convenience, or congeniality, weakened the church by dividing the people. We found it healthier and more faithful to set one service at the center of our life together, thereby declaring publicly that we are one people. That central service evolves gradually but constantly, with no intention of our achieving some final, fixed form. New elements are introduced or old ones returned rejuvenated not to *create* excitement by attracting attention to themselves, but because they *express* some excitement already felt and because they may help to reenact the gospel. That old hymn "Amazing Grace" found its way back, and people thought the words were newly written to tell how it is for them today.

A recent Youth Sunday service refreshed many an older person's faith not because the ordering of the worship conformed to custom or because the youth "performed" well, but because they witnessed to their experience of the gospel. If there was surprise when a girl spread her arms and fairly shouted "Wow" after a classmate spoke forthrightly about his recurrent need for pardon and confirmed the declaration of divine acceptance, that is because we are accustomed to respond with Doxology or Gloria. But the "Wow" was an appropriate reaction to divine surprise, undoubtedly a genuine expression of amazement and release for some who had grown up out of hearing of the church's alleluia.

A year ago on Memorial Sunday, as we were engaged in a churchwide study of church history, the communion meditation reflected on the great "cloud of witnesses." One witness after another was recalled through some telling human incident as the name was placed on the communion table: John Wright Buckham, twentieth-century theologian writing a now cherished hymn, "O God, Above the Drifting Years"; nineteenth-century New England laymen after the Civil War enabling their church to support schools and colleges for Negroes in the South; Martin Luther in the sixteenth century mourning his infant daughter; Polycarp, second-century bishop, speaking out for Christ in answer to Caesar's challenge. So the centuries were bridged. Then, card by card, we also placed there the names of our own dead since last Memorial Day: Walter Edmonds, Marian Hendrick, James Shelton. . . . As they were recalled, so Christ was recalled also. Here and there among the skeptics and believers people knew it was he who blessed and broke the bread and gave life.

Around this central service there are other ways of worship, rising and changing according to need but always with the intent of recalling Christ and being open to his presence.

The heart of this openness is in worship, but the end is not there. The entire experience in the church should be recognized as experience in Christ's presence and therefore instrumental and indeed essential in equipping God's people for work in his service. That service is to be in the world and all our struggles with diversity and ambiguity and perplexity within the church should be seen not as obstacles to but as preparation for such service. If we cannot let Christ deal with us as we are within the covenanted group, how can we presume to be his presence beyond it? Obedience presupposes openness.

The people of a local church are related by no other essential bond than Christ, whether they acknowledge him as personal Lord or have only been drawn to a body so committed. Life together within that covenant should consist in the faithful practice of acceptance, of caring, and of allowing ourselves to be cared for—surely no easy matter when we are not asked who the other members of this company shall be. It should breed that healing humor which can confess creatureliness with joy and acknowledge the Creator with praise.

If this is to be the nature of the community, it is also to be the content of Christian education. Experiencing, naming, appropriating, testing—these are steps whereby faith is born, identified, and nourished.

What a misunderstanding to think that Christian education is only what happens in precincts set apart for children's classrooms! Christian education is an unending, lifelong process which takes place whenever Christians meet. As for all the talk about curriculum centered in Bible, child, or church—folly! These elements cannot be torn apart to be arranged by either priority or logical sequence. They are threads, not foci, and inextricably interwoven in experience. The process takes place by inclusion and involvement of persons: children, great uncles, new members, church pillars, and all the rest in the total experience of the living, historical church. The church is indeed possessed of "tradition, book, and gospel" (chapter 3), but this lifeblood flows in living veins. The good news becomes concrete and specific in common experience. It is identified and related to the heritage in Sunday lessons. We cannot sit emotionally uninvolved to talk about acceptance. Acceptance is event, not theory. Acceptance happens when one person cares so much that he gives another person room and liberty to turn away in anger or in alienation. It happens when he still follows the absent one with that longing which refrains from touching but is waiting with a welcome when the prodigal returns. So we learn all the loaded, lovely language of religion. The words of sin, grace, redemption, rebirth, resurrection are labels we attach, identifying experience and thereby making it available to be recalled and recognized in life's next happening.

Identification of the happenings is living theology. The names are words the church has chosen—a private language, precious and pertinent. The events happen and are most readily recognized in an environment where trust runs high. This it is the church's task to provide from crib nursery to Friends in Retirement.

A group of church people have been coming together weekly, using a variety of books as prompters to search out one another's experience of life. Little by little these persons have grown to trust the group and its Christian context. Now, after a year and a half, dealing with *Death and Dying* (Elizabeth Kubler-Ross, Macmillan, 1969), they are taking new risks in looking at pain which has too long been festering behind the sort of stoic silence or tear-denying smile people call up when they have been misled into believing that grief is incompatible with faith.

The reenactment of the gospel, the opening of the gathered people to Christ's presence takes place in all areas of church life when the church is faithful. So by exposure and experience, God's people are equipped for his service.

THE RESPONSE

It was by just such a process of exposure and experience that Jesus equipped that first gathered band of a dozen to go out to be a Christian presence in their world. He likewise prepared the seventy and sent them. The church may well take note that these Christians were equipped in twofold fashion: with a spirit and with a mission. The spirit they gained from being with Jesus. The mission was their call to service. The intention of that mission was and is unmistakable.

People who have been with Christ are to be in the world as instruments for the world's redemption. Jesus put it straightforwardly: Tell the good news and heal the sick. In biblical terms the telling and the healing are in effect a single act. Word and deed are not separable. God speaks and it is so. We err by dividing them, being inclined either to mouth words without embodying them or to act without identifying our action with the divine Word. So we find good Christians bustling about performing acts of mercy or devoting all their eagerness and energy to social betterment, never conveying even by the sign of a shining countenance that there is great news abroad: it is the Lord himself who loves and lifts his people.

Jesus sent his disciples out stripped of every shred of external equipment they might use to insulate themselves from immediate and unadorned encounter with their fellow beings. He did not charge them to do good; he charged them to spread the word through their own being as they were inspired—enspirited—by his spirit. That spirit was their authority, the power which might move through them to drive out demons and to heal diseases. They were to take neither a packet of protective provisions nor a plan of procedure drawn from their limited wisdom and experience. Remember when those disciples were confronted with 5,000 people, surprised by nightfall far from their usual source of food? The only solution the twelve could propose was to send the people off into the dark and let each take care of himself. It was logical, of course, but it took no account at all of what might happen if the disciples themselves were to sit down there with the people, open to the Lord. It never occurred to them there might be some new, creative possibilities.

It is no different for us. It is not that the missionary barrel and the funds and the projects may not be appropriate and useful. It is that we lose touch with the source and think we are to build God's kingdom for him by our own power. Jesus insisted with his disciples that they belonged with the people. Join whatever householder will receive you. Earn your way, but work *with* people where they are. That is quite different from trying to work *on* them. So Rosemary Ruether writes: "The believers' church must recognize not only its continued solidarity with sinful humanity as its own lost brotherhood, but also its continued subservience to the mysteries of time and finitude as well." [1]

Two current experiences in the local church sharpen the point for us. The first is a shift in the nature of our youth work which we now understand as a major ministry of outreach of the church. The program centers in a remodeled house on the same block but not structurally connected with the church. Any youth is free to bring friends with a simple invitation to come to "our group," with or without naming the church. There is no program of indoctrination, but at times and in ways which seem appropriate the minister-leader presents himself, where he is in his own faith pilgrimage. He finds that this makes possible a continuing, honest dialogue which would never begin if someone did not open it out of his own integrity and which would die aborning if he indulged in dogmatism. Believers, seekers, and scorners meet in this place, exposed and vulnerable to one another. They are exposed also to the gospel as it is embodied there in a ministry of love for the youth, a self-offering of the church as an instrument of spiritual healing in a culture which is sick in its alienation. This missionary ministry is directed toward enabling youth to become whole persons, free to respond in their own honest way, whether by acceptance or rejection, to the good news proclaimed by the church. It is irrelevant to ask how many of these youth become involved in the church. Some do, others do not. The relevant question is the extent to which the church becomes present in (in-volved with!) this portion of the world. The program centers physically in "The House." It centers spiritually in the Lord.

A second current mission is the EAR, admittedly a minor address to the world but important in our learning. The EAR is a listening post for university students and others who may want a neutral listener to hear them out in some distress they are reluctant to expose to friends and relatives. The church members who make themselves available for this purpose have no advice to dispense, no funds to disburse, no program to follow. They are asked not to hide behind external para-phernalia but to be available as openly as possible to any visitor, to look with him at whatever he presents, and to respond to the person even though they may have no personal wisdom for dealing with the problem. Their equipment is to be their own encounter with the good news and such authority of spirit as they receive by being open to Christ's presence. The person who experiments with leaving cloak and bag behind soon discovers what a great risk he takes. Preparatory conversation among the listeners was stippled with words like "coffeepot," "telephone," and "easy chair"—clearly instruments to relieve their own anxiety. But EARs soon discovered that their visitors had more need for Kleenex than for coffee. No one, least of all Jesus, ever promised that honest encounter would be free of either pain or ambiguity.

THE RETURN

Obedience to Christ's spirit cannot be sustained without a regular rhythm of return to his presence. "On their return the apostles told Jesus all they had done; and he took them with him and withdrew privately (Luke 9:10, NEB [2]).'' The coming back is for both report and restoration. The inevitable wounds will fester in time and appear as bitterness and disillusionment if we do not submit now and then to the healing ministry of the church. Sooner or later energy will exhaust itself when ecstasy ebbs. The return and the drawing apart are also for discipline. Small groups gathered in Christ's name report what they have met "out there" in their experiences of rearing children or living with erratic youth or irritable aged, in trades and professions, in community service and political action, in acts of mercy, in spiritual witness and in the moral dilemmas not only of public responsibility but of private life as well. There may be both painful correction and amazing release when people probe experience together in faith and mutual acceptance.

Committees wrestling with problems of specific mission are powerful instruments of discipline. One such body, struggling month in, month out with an interracial undertaking, strained almost beyond endurance by internal tension, experienced the bite of the gospel in the heart of those meetings. Even before the project touched the community, committee members found that it was they who were in need of reconciliation and that by God's grace at least a little of their alienation was being overcome. Having set out to help, they soon discovered their own need of healing.

The going out and the coming back are not to be understood separately; they are phases of one motion like the crest and trough of a wave. It is artificial and indeed dangerous to divide church function into parish life and outreach. Persons who come together in Christ's name and who are open to his presence are both empowered and charged to be about his mission, embodying the good news in the world. They will return to report and to be drawn apart with Christ that he may refresh his spirit in them, thus sending them out once more.

EQUIPPED FOR SERVICE

Church calendars should be taken seriously. A church misses a fine instrument of teaching if its members or its visitors can read this schedule of activities as they would a prospectus for a county fair, hopefully with something to please everyone's fancy: Come see what you like, buy what you want, and skirt around the events and exhibits which threaten to disturb your holiday. The ritual of calendar headings is subject to change, and we might benefit by discontinuing altogether the columns long saved for "church school notes," "youth activities," "social concerns," and "women's work." It would be more faithful to the intention of the church for the calendar to show occasions for *gathering, self-opening, response,* and *return.* An enterprising editor will then translate these words into such captions as: Come One and All; Hear Ye, Hear Ye; Shine Forth; and Refreshment, Please. (An imaginative layman recently titled a "shine forth" section of this church's calendar "Un-bushel Your Beam"!) Any program element which does not fit appropriately under one of these headings should not be there at all.

These offerings will be functional even as we have proposed that a seminary curriculum must be functional. Intentional involvement in the church will begin with experiential participation in common worship through word and sacrament. It will include further:

Acceptance of responsibility to and for the community of faith, recognizing and rejoicing in the common humanity of all its members.

Commitment to evangelical ministry, a ministry of good news and redemption in a resistant, hurting, and alienated world.

123

Willingness to take risks.

Action, that is, Christian mission and ethical decision-making in some area of social life, coupled with reflection in company with fellow Christians in the church.

Development of personal skills for ministry.

Regular involvement with Christian tradition not as an intellectual exercise but in order to draw nourishment from the roots of faith.

Establishment of personal priorities in grateful response to the gospel.

The minister will be engaged with the people, enabling them in this process in order that, by God's grace, they may be an effective, redemptive presence in the world. Men and women who are drawn to Christ will be widely diverse and though they gather in his presence under one roof and are dispersed in one spirit they will perform their mission in an untold variety of ways.

Those persons who want the church to be a power block for unified action and to make a unified address to the world suffer endless frustration, because though the gospel is constant in intention, it neither stipulates nor encourages any fixed ritual for carrying out that purpose. Those who would choose ultimate independence in the exercise of faith, on the other hand, are likewise thwarted because there is in fact no way to know Christ at all except by way of the historical, experiencing community. As Christians we are bound to other Christians past and present through Jesus Christ. As local Christian churches we are bound to other Christian churches past and present through the same Lord. Our rituals will differ and change, our modes of mission will be various and always in process of forming and reforming; but our intention will be one: to be open to Christ's presence and obedient to his spirit.

NOTES

Introduction
1. P. T. Forsyth, *Congregationalism and Reunion* (London: Hazell, Watson & Viney, Ltd., 1952), p. 53.
2. Ibid.

Chapter 1. Retooling for a New Style
1. Ignazio Silone, *New Theology*, No. 1, p. 187.
2. J. S. Whale, *Christian Doctrine* (New York: Cambridge University Press, 1950), p. 128.
3. Peter Berger, *A Rumor of Angels* (New York: Doubleday, 1969), p. 121.
4. From the hymn "Praise, My Soul, the King of Heaven."
5. Robert N. Bellah, *Beyond Belief* (New York: Harper & Row, 1970), chap. 15.
6. Michael Polanyi, *Personal Knowledge* (Chicago: University of Chicago Press, 1958), p. 286.
7. J. B. Phillips (trans.), *Letters to Young Churches* (New York: Macmillan).

Chapter 2. Bury the Parish?
1. P. T. Forsyth, *The Church and the Sacraments* (London: Longmans, Green & Co., 1964; London: E. Baylas & Son, Ltd., The Trinity Press, 1917), p. 43.
2. Paul Tillich, *Systematic Theology* (Chicago: University of Chicago Press, 1963), III, 174.
3. Jaroslav Pelikan, *Obedient Rebels* (New York: Harper & Row, 1964), p. 15.

Chapter 3. The Spirit and the Strategy

1. Hans Küng, *The Church* (New York: Sheed & Ward, 1968), p. 85.
2. Author unknown.
3. Personal papers and communications from C. S. Cowles, formerly minister of First Church of the Nazarene, Atlanta, Georgia.
4. Ibid.

Chapter 4. Living in Style: Report from a Parish Church

1. Milton Rokeach, *Value Survey*, 1967.
2. Browne Barr, "A Pastoral Letter," *The Carillon*, March 1, 1970.

Chapter 5. Pop Sermons

1. Justus George Lawler, "Theology and the Uses of History," *Continuum*, Spring 1966; reprinted in *New Theology*, No. 4. Used by permission of the author.
2. Ibid.
3. Ibid.

Chapter 6. Sermon Seminar

1. The application of this principle in the local congregation has been set forth in a study by Dietrich Ritschl, *A Theology of Proclamation* (Richmond: John Knox Press, 1960).

Chapter 7. Beyond Activism

1. Langdon Gilkey, "Social and Intellectual Sources of Contemporary Protestant Theology." Reprinted by permission of *Daedalus*, Journal of the American Academy of Arts and Sciences, Boston, Mass., Winter 1967, *Religion in America*.
2. Ibid.
3. Michael Harrington, quoted in Schubert M. Ogden, "How Does God Function in Human Life?" *Christianity and Crisis*, May 1967, p. 105.
4. *The Church for Others: Two Reports on the Missionary Structure of the Congregation*, ed. Walter J. Hollenweger (Geneva: World Council of Churches, 1967), p. 4. Used by permission.
5. Ibid.
6. Ibid., p. 126.
7. Ibid.
8. Ibid.

Chapter 8. Education for Ministry in the Local Church

1. Michael Novak, "Healing Class Tensions in a Sick Society," *Christianity and Crisis*, June 8, 1970 (italics added).

126

2. Cynthia Wedel, *The Christian Century*, August 12, 1970.

3. Hans Küng, *The Church* (New York: Sheed & Ward, 1968), p. 85.

4. Robert Rubin, *San Francisco Chronicle*, August 4, 1970.

Chapter 9. To Equip God's People for Work in His Service

1. Rosemary Ruether, The Chicago Theological Seminary *Register*, Sept. 1970, Vol. 60, No. 6, p. 8.

2. From *The New English Bible, New Testament.* © The Delegates of the Oxford University Press and the Syndics of the Cambridge University Press 1961. Reprinted by permission.